Becky May has led various children's and youth groups and programmes over the past 20 years, including Sunday morning discipleship groups for children aged 0–12 and midweek outreach groups for both primary-age children and teenagers. She was a primary school teacher for eight years, teaching in both Key Stage 1 and 2 and fulfilling leadership responsibilities, before leaving teaching to have her son, Isaac, in September 2012. More recently, the family has grown again following the arrival of baby Keziah. She has written for *Youthwork* magazine, YFC, Urban Saints, UCB and One Way UK, creating a variety of curriculum materials, articles, children's devotional materials and assembly scripts. Becky is also the Bedfordshire Regional Coordinator for Messy Church and cofounder of The Treasurebox People.

Published by
The Bible Reading Fellowship (BRF)
15 The Chambers, Vineyard
Abingdon OX14 3FE
United Kingdom
Tel: +44 (0)1865 319700
Email: enquiries@brf.org.uk
Website: www.brf.org.uk
BRF is a Registered Charity

ISBN 978 0 85746 426 2

First published 2016
10 9 8 7 6 5 4 3 2 1 0

Acknowledgements
Cover photo: © Thinkstock

Every effort has been made to trace and contact copyright owners for material used in this resource. We apologise for any inadvertent omissions or errors, and would ask those concerned to contact us so that full acknowledgement can be made in the future.

A catalogue record for this book is available from the British Library

Printed by Gutenberg Press, Tarxien, Malta

Important information

Photocopying permission

The right to photocopy material in *God's Story for 7–11s* is granted for the pages that contain the photocopying clause: 'Reproduced with permission from *God's Story for 7–11s* by Becky May (Barnabas for Children, 2016) www.barnabasinchurches.org.uk', so long as reproduction is for use in a teaching situation by the original purchaser. The right to photocopy material is not granted for anyone other than the original purchaser without written permission from BRF.

The Copyright Licensing Agency (CLA)

If you are resident in the UK and you have a photocopying licence with the Copyright Licensing Agency (CLA) please check the terms of your licence. If your photocopying request falls within the terms of your licence, you may proceed without seeking further permission. If your request exceeds the terms of your CLA licence, please contact the CLA directly with your request. Copyright Licensing Agency, Saffron House, 6–10 Kirby Street, London EC1N 8TS UK, Tel: 020 7400 3100, email cla@cla.co.uk; web www.cla.co.uk. The CLA will provide photocopying authorisation and royalty fee information on behalf of BRF.

The Bible Reading Fellowship (BRF) is a Registered Charity (233280).

Becky May

GOD'S STORY FOR 7–11s

36 Bible-based sessions for midweek and Sunday groups

Contents

Old Testament stories

New Testament stories

Introduction

This is the third and final book in a series exploring many of the key events from God's story, through a creative and diverse curriculum, with activities designed to meet the needs of children with a range of learning styles. Together with the curriculum for under 5-year-olds and 5- to 7-year-olds, this book completes the set, providing age-appropriate activities and ideas for 7- to 11-year-olds.

Who is this book for?

This curriculum has been prepared for anybody who wants to share God's big story with children aged 7–11. It could be used as a year-long programme to work through the big story of the Bible week by week, throughout the academic year, or the appropriate stories may be used to celebrate key festivals in the church calendar, with other sessions slotted in as best suits your teaching plan for the year.

It can be used both in a midweek children's group and a Sunday morning group, perhaps alongside the main church services. For smaller, mixed age groups, you may find it helpful to use some of the activities contained within this book alongside those suggested in the other two books in the series, to create a programme that works well for your particular group.

The 36 sessions, which run in sequence, work together to tell God's big story from creation to Pentecost. Within one academic year, there is not time to explore the whole Bible, so this book contains a selection of key stories from both the Old and New Testaments.

Story time

For this age group (unlike the books for younger children), the story has been placed at the beginning of the session, with a range of related activities suggested to follow on from it. However, you may prefer to share the story after you have completed the other activities, depending upon the needs of your children and your own preferred teaching style.

Suggestions are made about how to read or tell the story. They often involve a small group reading the Bible together or enacting the story through drama activities, as described below, but there are occasions when other means are used to tell and explore the story together. In addition, you will find a number of open-ended questions to use as discussion starters with the children. They are by no means exhaustive and are intended to provide children with a starting point for thinking and discussing some of the things that we can learn from the story. You will also find key points required for explanation and further points for the children's own personal reflection and application.

Activity areas

Each of the 36 sessions explores the story and themes through a selection of different activities. These meet the needs of children with a number of different learning styles and preferences, and of different ages and abilities. Where you have time, space and available adults to support the children's learning, the curriculum works best if all activities can be prepared and set up for the children to explore. For smaller groups, or those with other constraints on resources, try to provide a variety and range of activities that meet the needs of all the children, choosing from the activities described below, perhaps from different categories each session.

The drama activity or a group discussion could be completed by the whole group together at the start of the session, to share the theme and set the scene for further learning and exploration through a range of other activities. It is suggested that the other activities are set up to run simultaneously, allowing the children to choose which activities to engage with in the time given. At the end, there is an opportunity to bring the group back together as you draw things to a close.

Included with the activities are a selection of things that adult helpers can talk about with the children as they complete the tasks. If you have enough helpers available, an adult could work alongside the children at every station. If this is not the case, you could either talk to the children at specific activity areas or create space within the group time at the end of the session to explore some of the ideas and questions raised.

Below you will find a short explanation of each activity area, with instructions on how to set up the environment for the best possible outcome.

Drama

These activities often offer a suggestion about how the children can re-enact the Bible story, using a variety of simple drama techniques. At other times, the activities provide an opportunity to explore some of the wider themes found within the Bible story, in a way which relates more to the children's own experiences, encouraging them to think about how to apply the lessons they learn from the story.

ICT

These activities make use of a range of ICT techniques, many of which will be familiar to the children. The activities require a few widely available resources, such as a laptop or tablet with access to the internet, with only a few other easy-to-source pieces of equipment and no expensive software programmes. You will need to ensure that the children understand how to work safely when accessing the internet.

Creative

The activities suggested here make use of a wide variety of artistic techniques, materials and equipment. Some of the activities are designed for collaborative work, perhaps to create something for use elsewhere in the sessions, while others enable the children to make something to take away with them as a reminder of the session or the themes explored.

Construction

Many of the suggested construction activities enable the children to work together as a team to create something on a larger scale. These activities could be carried out in small competing teams or as a whole-group collaboration. There are also opportunities for individual construction. The construction activities make use of different materials, tools and techniques and will often require adult supervision to ensure the children's safe working.

Writing

The suggested writing activities offer a quiet, reflective, individual activity for the children to engage with, alongside the more active and collaborative activities suggested elsewhere. A 'quiet table' with the required resources will be needed, as well as support for children who have difficulty in writing but choose to engage with this activity.

Books

Each session outline suggests a number of themes that can be explored in a selection of books. These could include Bibles and books that retell the story, alongside other related Bible stories with which the children can make connections and discover more about the related themes of the session. A reading area, perhaps with a rug, cushions or beanbags, would help to make this activity appealing and accessible for the group.

Prayer and reflective activity

These activities are adult-led, offering a significant opportunity to discuss the teaching of the session and to raise issues or questions in greater depth. They also provide children with a creative opportunity to respond to the teaching of the session at a personal level, perhaps through personal prayer or a practical application to their own daily lives.

Games

Most of the suggested games are large and active, including team games and well-known playground games. Some simple items of equipment will be required, alongside a large playing space. On other occasions, suggestions are made for board games that children can play together in smaller groups.

Challenge

These activities involve an element of problem solving or competition, sometimes taking the form of an extra game or construction activity. They offer a combination of collaborative and individual ways to engage and respond.

Prayer

A short concluding prayer is offered, which draws together the key learning points of the session and provides children with an opportunity to respond in a simple way. You may find it helpful to introduce the prayer by saying, 'I'm going to say a prayer. Please listen carefully and, if you want to join in, you can say "Amen" at the end.'

Songs

For each session, one or two songs are suggested, which can be sung together, either with a live musician leading or with backing track recordings. A number of the songs make use of simple actions for the children to learn and use. You may also need to think about projecting the words for children to follow.

Take home

At the close of each session, a suggestion is made for something that the children can do in the following week to put into practice or further explore the themes of the session. It might involve encouraging the children to take home something that they have made, or to go away and find out something new. There are times when you may find it helpful to recap in the following session, inviting the children to share what they have learnt or raise any further questions they may have, continuing the discipling journey.

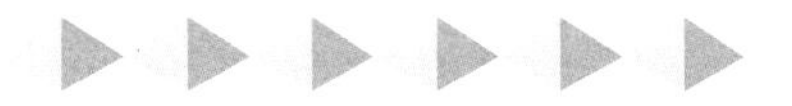

Old Testament stories

1

God creates the world

For the team

Refer to pages 6–9 to see how the activity areas work together

Session theme

This session explores the very beginning of God's big story—the creation of the world. We will celebrate the great diversity of the created world and think about how we can take our responsibility seriously to look after the world that God has made.

Bible text: Genesis 1—2

Team prayer

Creator God, thank you for your great creation which you have invited us to enjoy. Thank you, too, for the gifts of creativity which you share with us. Help us to use these gifts to further your kingdom. Amen

Story time

Share the story together, either from an age-appropriate children's Bible story book, or from an appropriate translation. This can be done as a separate exercise or as you complete the drama activity, as described below.

- How well did you know this story?
- What did you notice for the first time?
- What surprises you about this story?
- Do you have any questions about the story of creation?

Talk about the issues and questions raised by the story. Help the children to recognise that many things in the Bible are not easy to understand, even for adults, but we can bring our questions back to God, trying to grasp more fully the things that he wants to teach us. Remind the children that when God first created the world, everything was perfect and people lived in relationship with God, just as he wanted it to be. This was the very start of a big story, in which people's relationships with God change, but his love for them never goes away.

Say: Did you know that the Bible says that you are 'fearfully and wonderfully made' (Psalm 139:14)? Just as God was very pleased with Adam and Eve when they were first created, God smiles when he looks at you. He loves you as part of his beautiful creation; how does that make you feel?

Activity areas

Drama

Divide the children into smaller groups and assign one day of the creation story to each small group. Provide Bibles or copies of the story, and ask the children to create a short mime to represent what happened on the day that they have been given.

Talk about the children's own ideas about how they can visually represent the different elements of God's creation and what important details they should include. Encourage them to use their whole bodies and to work together as a group in the movements they make.

Talk together about any questions, ideas or issues raised by this activity.

ICT

Provide safe access to the internet on computers, laptops or tablets and have a number of strips of coloured paper available along with felt pens. Invite the children to spend time finding out about their favourite elements of God's incredible world (this could be looking up their favourite animal or things about space; whatever they are particularly interested in). The children should then write down their favourite short fact on a strip of paper before displaying it where everybody can see it.

Talk about the fascinating facts that the children discover and why they are of interest to them.

Creative

Gather some old (unwanted) clothes, as well as newspapers and carrier bags, to use for stuffing. Work together with the children to create large stuffed animals from different parts of the clothes (sleeves make great legs, long necks or even trunks). The clothing items can be put together with a stapler, if you prefer not to sew.

Talk about the children's favourite animals. What do you notice about their different shapes and sizes?

Construction

Source an old or unwanted piece of furniture, such as a table or chair, and provide a selection of materials needed to upcycle the item. These could include appropriate paints and fabrics, along with sandpaper and a selection of tools. Invite the children to work together to improve the state of the item provided, repairing any damage and improving its overall appearance.

Talk about the way that God gave human beings responsibility to care for his creation. Do we always make best use of the resources we have available to us or do we sometimes waste what we have? How can we better care for the planet?

Writing

Prepare some basic shapes of easily recognisable things from God's creation, cut from coloured paper. These could include birds, fish, flowers, and so on. Invite the children to write their own 'shape poems', writing lines that describe their chosen item inside the shape. The lines do not need to rhyme, and they could be as simple as a list of adjectives.

Talk about what makes each of these things special and unique and how we can thank God for the diversity that we see in his creation.

Books

Provide age-appropriate books telling the creation story, along with children's Bibles. You could also offer age-appropriate books about each aspect of creation, including different people groups or tribes, animals, birds, plants, oceans and space.

Talk about the things that interest the children when they look at the books, as appropriate, and be available to support those less able to read independently.

Prayer and reflective activity

Take the children out into the local area with a digital camera and invite them to take photographs of the things they see that they most love about God's creation. When you return to the main venue, display these images using a laptop and projector for everyone to see, perhaps playing the images on a loop while you play some reflective music.

Talk about the different things that children choose as you are out and about and how we can see beauty and creativity all around us, if we open our eyes to see them.

Games

Set up a treasure hunt in which you hide pictures or small objects relating to each day of the creation story. At the appropriate time, challenge the children, perhaps in smaller teams (in which case you will need multiple sets of objects), to find each of the images and to arrange them in order to retell the story of creation.

Prayer

Creator God, thank you that you created a beautiful world where we could live as your friends. Thank you for all the many things you gave us to enjoy. Help us to be good stewards, taking care of the world that you have made. Amen

Songs

Songs today could include:

- 'God's love is so big' (Simon Parry)
- 'On the first day' (Dave Godfrey)

Take home

Suggest to the children that they take some time each day in the week ahead to thank God for one thing that they love about the created world.

2

Adam and Eve make a bad choice

For the team

Refer to pages 6–9 to see how the activity areas work together

Session theme

During this session, we discover how God's perfect created world was spoiled by one bad decision. We think about the story of Adam, Eve and a serpent, but also think about the choices that we make, and how God gives us the opportunity to start again when we get things wrong.

Bible text: Genesis 3

Team prayer

Father God, we are sorry for the times when we make bad decisions and do things that do not honour you. Help us to share, honestly, what it means to try to follow your ways while knowing that you always give us a fresh start when we do things wrong. Amen

Story time

As a group, look together at Genesis 3, either in an age-appropriate retelling, or in a children's story Bible.

- How does this story make you feel?
- Does anything about this story surprise you?
- Why do you think things happened this way?
- What else do we know about today that gives us hope?

Say: We like stories to have happy endings. During the last session, we enjoyed everything that God had made in his beautiful world, but today we discover how things went wrong. God was very sad when Adam and Eve chose to do the wrong thing, just as he is sad when we do things wrong today. But we know this is not the end of the story. God still loved his people and would make a way for them to be his friends once again. But after this day, things would always be different and God's perfect world would never be quite so perfect again.

Say: I wonder what advice you might give Eve and Adam when they were given a choice. It's easy for us to see what they did wrong, but sometimes we make bad choices too. Remember that God still loves us and wants to give us a fresh start, no matter what we do wrong.

Drama

Write out a few different scenarios on small pieces of paper and invite the children to work together to act these out, thinking about the dilemma they are faced with and how they might respond. Each of the scenarios should give the children a choice to make about how they should or would act if they found themselves in that particular situation. For example, if you're asked to take care of a new child at school, but your friends want you to play with them instead, or if you borrow your friend's favourite DVD and it gets broken while in your care.

Talk about each of the scenarios as the children act them out and discuss each of the options available to them. Try not to guide their decision-making, but rather ask questions which help them to think about all the options available to them; what they think they should do, and what they think they are most likely to do. Adam and Eve had a choice to make when the serpent tried to tempt them. What do you think you would do in that situation?

Creative

Cut the legs off of some old pairs of thick, coloured, children's tights and invite the children to use them to make a snake. Cheap pillow stuffing can be used to stuff the body of the snake, before sewing the end closed and decorating the snake with fabric scraps in assorted colours.

Talk about the way that the snake is portrayed as the villain in the story and blamed for everything that goes wrong, but that actually Adam and Eve each had a choice to make for themselves, and they chose to do the one thing God had told them not to do.

Construction

Work together with the children to construct a large model gateway, perhaps nailing pieces of wood together, glueing thick card or even constructing a gate from pieces of metal if you have a helper available with the appropriate skills and tools.

Talk about the way that gateways often symbolise an entrance into something. What did it mean for God to close the gate on Adam and Eve? How do you think they would have felt when this happened?

Writing

Provide a selection of small notecards and pens and invite the children, if they wish, to write a short message to somebody they feel they need to apologise to. Provide envelopes for the children to put their cards in, ready to give to the person they are addressed to.

Talk about any issues that this activity raises, as appropriate. Discuss the fact that we cannot undo the bad decisions that we make, but we can apologise when we hurt or upset somebody and try to make things right again.

Books

Display a selection of children's Bibles and books which tell the story of Adam and Eve. You could also provide the same selection of non-fiction books about aspects of creation from the previous session.

Share the books with the children, supporting them with reading as appropriate. Talk about the way that we can still enjoy God's creation, even though it was damaged when human beings began to make bad choices.

Prayer and reflective activity

Provide paper and pens and set up an electronic shredder under adult supervision. Invite the children to write short 'sorry' prayers on the paper provided, thinking of something they want to say sorry to God for, before putting the paper through the shredder.

Talk about the way that we mess up and get things wrong, just as Adam and Eve did. God had to take them away from the special place that he had created for them, but he still wanted to have a relationship with them. God wants to forgive us for the wrong things we do; getting rid of them in the shredder gives us a brand new start.

Games

Play some games which involve the children making choices. This could be tactical games, such as chess, or a group game, such as 'would you rather', where the children make a choice about which of two given options they would rather accept, and vote by moving to one side of the room or the other to indicate their vote. Examples of questions that could be used include: would you rather be a bird or a mouse? Would you rather bath in treacle or yogurt? and so on.

Prayer

Father God, we are sorry for the times when we make bad choices, like Adam and Eve did. Thank you that you give us a fresh start every time we say we are sorry, so that we can be close to you again. Amen

Songs

Songs today could include:

- 'If I've been wrong' (Sammy Horner)

Take home

Challenge the children to think about whether there is someone they need to apologise to this week for the things they may have done. Or perhaps they need to think really carefully, when they are given a choice, about the things they say or do.

3

Noah and the ark

For the team

Refer to pages 6–9 to see how the activity areas work together

Session theme

During this session, we consider this well-known story and think about the costly decision that God made to flood the earth and start again. We also look at the promise he made never to flood the earth again, and explore some of the other promises that can be found in the Bible.

Bible text: Genesis 6—9

Team prayer

Creator God, thank you that you are the God of fresh starts. Help us today, as we reflect on this story, to share something fresh and new with the children with whom we work, so that they may discover more of the promises of God. Amen

Story time

Share the story together, perhaps from an age-appropriate children's Bible or from a story book. You could do this as you prepare the freeze frames in the drama activity, as described below, or as a separate activity.

- How do feel about this story?
- What is your favourite part of the story and why?
- What do you imagine things would have been like for Noah? For God?
- What does this story tell us about God?

Explain to the children that this is one of the most well-known Bible stories, but we often think about it as a boat full of cute and fluffy animals, floating along as the rain fell down. The reality is that this is a really difficult story to understand. God chose to destroy everything that he had made because things had become so bad. Noah had to stand up to people, even when they were laughing at him, to do what God had told him to do, and his family were the only ones to put God first. In this story, we think about the way that God gave the whole earth a brand new start at a great cost. This wouldn't be the last time that people did wrong things, but it would be the last time that God would send a flood, and one day he would give all people a brand new fresh start.

Say: I wonder whether you think God should have sent the flood. This is a tough story for us to understand, but God still showed that he loved his people and wanted the best for them, just as he wants for us today.

Drama

Divide the children into smaller groups, and assign one scene from the story to each group, asking them to create a freeze frame showing what happened in that scene. Provide Bibles or copies of the story for children to look at as they decide what to include. The stages of the story could include:

- What God saw when he looked at the world
- Noah building the ark
- The animals arrive
- Life on the ark
- Leaving the ark

Once the children have had time to put their freeze frames together, invite each group to perform their scene. As they do so, tap performers on the shoulder, one at a time, and ask them: 'How do you feel at this point?' 'What are you thinking, right now?' or 'What do you think you would say now?'

Talk about the children's responses to the questions. How do these things help us to think about the story and the characters involved?

ICT

Provide safe access to the internet on laptops or tablets, and invite the children to create a size comparison image.

Find out the size of the ark, according to the measurements given in the Bible. (Make sure you use a Bible translation such as the Contemporary English Version, which gives modern measurements.) Generate a list of well-known objects to use as comparisons, such as the Eiffel Tower, the *Titanic* and a football stadium, and search online to discover their dimensions. Children can copy images of these images and then resize them so that they are approximately in proportion to the ark.

Talk about the way Noah's ark was built, at a time when nobody would have seen such a large structure. How surprised would people have been to see the ark taking shape?

Creative

Provide some modelling clay and invite the children to create a small clay sculpture of anything they wish. Encourage the children to take their time and create a detailed sculpture.

Talk about how God took time creating his beautiful world and how he loved all that he had made. Ask the children how they would feel to crush or destroy their models now. How do you think God felt when he had to destroy his beautiful creation by sending the flood?

Construction

Provide measuring equipment, such as a trundle wheel, and take the children into the local area to measure out how large the ark would have been, according to the measurements given in the Bible.

Talk about how Noah followed God's instructions to build the ark to the correct measurements.

Writing

Provide access to Bibles and a concordance, or an online Bible with a search tool, and show the children how to search a thematic or topical index to look up God's promises, to find other examples of promises that God has made to his people. Encourage the children to write out any that strike a chord with them, to make a small display.

Talk about the different promises that the children find and what they mean for us today. Remind the children that God always keeps his promises and can always be trusted.

Books

Along with age-appropriate books of this story and children's Bibles, you could also provide a selection of non-fiction books with themes of animals and weather.

Talk about the things that interest the children when they look at the books, as appropriate, and be available to support those less able to read independently.

Prayer and reflective activity

Source a number of small glass prisms which the children can experiment with, together with a small safe light source, such as a small torch. Encourage the children to look closely at the rainbows they can create and the different colours that appear in each one.

Talk about the rainbows we still see today when we have sun and rain together, which remind us of God's promise never to flood the earth again.

Challenge

Provide small pictures or models of a number of different animals and a large sheet of paper with the outline of the ark drawn on it. Invite the children to order the animals on the ark drawing to show how they would position the animals if they were in charge of the ark.

Talk about the way that the children solve this problem and the sequence they use, drawing attention to any 'known enemies' that they may have placed too close to one another. How difficult do they think it would have been for Noah to ensure that all the animals were safe on board the ark?

Prayer

Father God, we are sorry for the times when we do things we know we shouldn't do. Help us to be more like Noah, following your instructions and trusting you, even when it is the difficult thing to do. Amen

Songs

Songs today could include:

- 'Rainbow' (David and Beci Wakerly)

Take home

Encourage the children to take home some of the promises God has made to us, that they found in the writing activity, and to display these somewhere in their homes as a reminder of the things that God has promised them.

4 God's promise to Abraham and Sarah

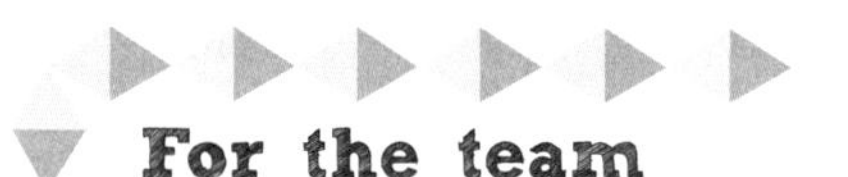

For the team

Refer to pages 6–9 to see how the activity areas work together

Session theme

This session explores how Abraham and Sarah waited a whole lifetime for God to give them their long-promised son, Isaac. The timescale involved, and the long-held desire for a baby, are abstract themes to explore with the children, but this session focuses on what it means for God to keep his promises, no matter how long we have to wait.

Bible text: Genesis 15; 17:1—18:15; 21:1–7

Team prayer

Father God, thank you that when you make a promise it will always come into being. Help us to understand the times that we need to wait for your promises to be fulfilled, as you know what is best for us, and your timing will always be right. Amen

Story time

Today's story is found in a number of separate passages, describing different episodes. You may wish to summarise some of the story in your own words before looking, perhaps, at the passages in Genesis 18 and Genesis 21:1–7 in an easy-to-read Bible translation.

- What did you enjoy most about this story?
- What surprised you?
- Can you imagine how Abraham and Sarah would have felt at each stage of events?
- What can we learn about God from this tale?

Help the children to understand the massive timescale involved in this story and how long Abraham and Sarah had to wait for their promised child, perhaps relating it to the ages of people in their own families or within your community.

Say: I wonder how long you've had to wait for something that was promised to you, perhaps a Christmas present or a holiday trip. Sarah and Abraham waited many, many years for God to give them a son, and they could be forgiven for the times when they doubted whether it would ever happen. I wonder whether we have had to wait for God to answer any of our prayers. God's plans are always best for us. We may need to wait sometimes, and we may not understand why, but God works all things together for our good.

You may need to create space to discuss any particular questions or issues raised by this story and discussion, later in the session.

Activity areas

Drama

Set up a chair as a hot seat and invite volunteers to play the parts of Abraham and Sarah. Model how to interview the person sitting in the hot seat, to find out more about how they acted, and how they felt about what happened to them as the story unfolded. Invite the other children to ask their own questions of Abraham and Sarah, as they become more confident. This activity could be repeated with other children playing the main characters, as time allows.

Talk about Abraham's and Sarah's responses to the questions asked. How does thinking of them as real people help us to better understand the surprising events of this story?

ICT

Provide laptops or tablets and access to the internet and invite the children to research the meanings of their own names, the names of their family members and of the helpers present. Encourage the children to look at more than one source to check for reliability.

Talk about how God told Abraham to call his son Isaac, meaning laughter. Names are very significant in many Bible stories; there are other stories about times when God told a parent what name to give their child or changed a person's name as a sign of a new beginning.

Creative

Provide some small bottles and sand in a variety of colours and invite the children to fill their own sand bottle, creating a pattern as they do so. (Craft kits can be purchased for this purpose, or you can colour sand yourself with chalk powder.) Ensure that the bottles are filled with sand and sealed securely to avoid any spillages.

Talk about God's promise to Abraham that his descendants would outnumber the grains of sand on the shore. Ask the children how many grains of sand they can count in their bottle. What do they think Abraham would have understood by God's promise?

Construction

Provide some tents, appropriate to the size of your venue, which the children can work together to construct, following the instructions provided. Let the children take a lead in the construction process, providing support as needed.

Talk about how our modern-day tents are different from those which Abraham and Sarah would have been familiar with. Could they imagine living in a tent all the time?

Writing

Provide paper and pens or pencils and invite the children to write a short diary or journal entry as though they were either Abraham or Sarah, reflecting at the end of the day when the visitors came.

Talk about how Abraham and Sarah must have felt that day. What lasting memories would they have held on to? They would not really have written these things down, but they would never forget how they felt at the end of that day.

Books

Provide a selection of children's Bibles and stories about Abraham, Sarah and Isaac. You could also provide some age-appropriate testimonies by people who have demonstrated trust in God, regardless of their own situation.

Talk about the things that interest the children when they look at the books, as appropriate, and be available to support those less able to read independently.

Prayer and reflective activity

Provide large sand timers and encourage the children to sit quietly and watch as the grains of sand flow through them.

Talk about the way that Abraham and Sarah had to wait a long time for God to honour his promise and how they could be forgiven for the times when they doubted whether it would ever happen. Share your own stories of times when you have had to wait for God to answer your prayers. Do the children have their own stories to share too?

Games

Set up two shallow sand trays with plastic stars hidden under the sand (at least as many stars as there are children in your group). Divide the group into two teams for a relay race. In turn, players run to the tray, find one star and return to the group. The winning team is the one to find all their stars first.

Challenge

Print out some recognised star constellations, or recreate them using star-shaped stickers on black card. Challenge the children to identify them by their known names or to create their own constellation names for the star patterns, based on the pictures they can see in the patterns.

Talk about the constellation names and how God set each star into place. This same God, who created the vast universe, cared about Abraham and Sarah and their longing for a child of their own.

Prayer

Father God, thank you that you always keep your promises, just as you did for Abraham and Sarah. Help us to trust you, even when we cannot see or understand what is happening, because you have the best plans for our lives. Amen

Songs

Songs today could include:

- 'Father Abraham' (Anon)

Take home

Suggest to the children that when they get home, they could ask about the name meanings of different members of their own family, and find out how and why those names were chosen.

Joseph is taken to Egypt

For the team

Refer to pages 6–9 to see how the activity areas work together

Session theme

This session is the first of two, exploring the life of Joseph. In this session, we consider the difficult relationships within his family and how this led to his departure to Egypt. Through this session, we will think about our own family relationships and the role that we play in keeping these relationships healthy and positive.

Bible text: Genesis 37

Team prayer

Father God, thank you for our families, in which you have chosen to place us. As we work with children today from a wide variety of family backgrounds and situations, may we share your father heart for them all, and help them to build positive relationships within their family groups. Amen

Story time

For today's retelling of the story, provide printouts of the story and highlighter pens in three different colours. As you read through Genesis 37 together, encourage the children to highlight the things that Joseph did in one colour, the things his brothers did in a second colour and the things that Jacob did in the third colour. Talk about the issues raised by doing this and how it helps us to look more closely at the way that each of the characters acted in this situation.

- How do you feel about each of the characters now we have looked at the story in this way?
- What surprises you about the story?
- How do you think the different characters would have felt at each stage of the story?
- How do you think they would have felt after Joseph had gone away?

Remind the children that we often think of Joseph as the victim in this story, and ultimately he was, but looking more closely at the things he said and did helps us to understand more about his relationship with his siblings and why things started to go wrong.

Say: I wonder what God wanted Jacob, Joseph and his brothers to learn as a family. I wonder what this story can teach us about how we act towards our own families. Joseph had a special gift from God from a very early age, but he was also a human being just like you and me and he didn't always act in the best way possible. Some of the things he said and did caused hurt to others and soured his relationships. God loves each of us equally, just as he loves our parents and our brothers and sisters. How can we show more love to one another?

Drama

Assign different roles from the story to each child: Jacob, Joseph and each of his brothers. Provide copies of the story, or children's Bibles, and ask the children to find out more about the different characters that they are to play.

Ask the remaining children to play the part of detectives, asking questions of the other children 'in role' (similar to those asked in a hot-seating activity), to try to find out how things went wrong for Joseph and how he ended up being sold into slavery.

Talk about each of the characters, what the children find out about them and the part they played in the story. Who should take responsibility for what happened to Joseph? How did things reach this stage?

ICT

Set up access to a drawing or design programme and invite the children to design their own brightly coloured and patterned coat. Some design programmes enable you to set up a template, so you can provide a basic coat shape for the children to fill with their design. You could print out the completed designs to create a display.

Talk about the different designs that the children use and how they came to decide upon them. Joseph's coat was a special gift from his father; what special gifts have we received from our family? Why do they matter so much to us?

Creative

Gather some old, unwanted coats or shirts and a selection of brightly coloured fabric scraps, fabric glue, fabric paints or pens and invite the children to use the materials to customise their own coat for Joseph, perhaps working in pairs or small groups.

Talk about the different designs that the children choose. How much care and attention do you think went into Jacob's coat for his son? Why is this coat so central to the story?

Construction

Provide a selection of junk modelling materials, including cardboard boxes, tubes and other packaging materials. Challenge the children to construct the most convincing camel that they can from the materials provided. For larger groups, this could be held as a contest in teams, while smaller groups could work together to create one camel.

Talk about how Joseph was taken to Egypt by the traders who travelled past Joseph's brothers when they were deciding what to do with him. How must he have felt being taken away by strangers to an unfamiliar land?

Writing

Provide a selection of plain postcards which the children can decorate, or some postcards with pictures of Egypt and the Holy Land. Invite the children to write a message from Joseph to his father or from Jacob to his son, as though they were able to make contact with each other for the first time.

Talk about the way that, once they had been separated, Jacob and Joseph had no means of getting in touch with one another again, but that they probably often thought of what they would like to say, if they had had the opportunity.

Books

The selection of books offered today should include children's Bibles and stories about Joseph and his life. You could also include a selection of non-fiction books about Ancient Egypt and stories about families.

Talk about the things that interest the children when they look at the books, as appropriate, and be available to support those less able to read independently.

Prayer and reflective activity

In advance, ask the children to bring photos of their families with them to the session. Create a display of all the photos. Pray for each of the families represented within the group, praying specifically for any known issues or situations, or using a general prayer for God's blessing over each family.

Talk about how each of our families is different and unique, but that they are special to us. We often have problems to resolve in families, perhaps times when we argue with our brothers and sisters, but we still love them, and can thank God for the way he looks after us within our family groups.

Games

You could set up a camel relay race today, with children working in pairs, with an older, stronger child giving a piggyback to a smaller child, as a reminder of the way that Joseph was taken as a slave to Egypt.

You will need to ensure that this activity is completed under supervision, with children who are old enough to carry one another safely.

Prayer

Father God, thank you that we are all your children, known and loved by you, in spite of our faults. Help us to show love to other people, especially within our own families, and to remember that you love us all the same. Amen

Songs

Songs today could include:

- 'Brother Joe' (Dave Godfrey)

Take home

Challenge the children to think about their brothers and sisters, or other family members, this week. How can they put other people's needs first? Perhaps they could play a game with a younger sibling, or help their parents with some chores without being asked.

6 Joseph serves God

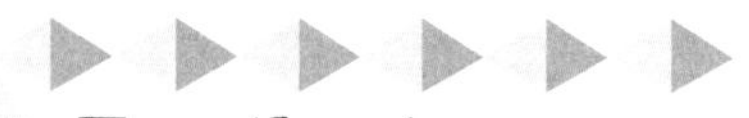

For the team

Refer to pages 6–9 to see how the activity areas work together

Session theme

This is the second of two sessions, exploring the life of Joseph and looking at how the interpreter of dreams was raised up from his place as a prisoner to second-in-command to the Pharaoh. Through this session, we think about how we can trust God to care for us, just as he cared for Joseph, regardless of our position or circumstances, knowing that God is with us in the high points as well as when life is challenging.

Bible text: Genesis 39—45

Team prayer

Almighty God, you are with us in every circumstance and situation. Help us to remember that you will protect us from harm, and to look for you, whatever situation we are facing. Amen

Story time

Today's story covers a number of episodes from Joseph's life, beginning with his arrival in Egypt, leading to the reunion of the family in Genesis 45. It may work well to explore the story in a series of episodes, perhaps in small groups, dividing the passage as described in the drama activity below. Each group could then share their particular section with the wider group, in sequence.

- What did you enjoy about the story?
- What surprised you about the story?
- What do you think Joseph learned from his different experiences?
- How did God look after Joseph in each circumstance?

Remind the children that this is a story which took place over many years, in a range of different circumstances and situations. Through all of these, God was both looking after Joseph and helping him to grow and change, ready for the next stage of his life.

Say: I wonder how much more we would understand about Joseph and how he felt in each circumstance, if we could see inside his head. I wonder if he could always see God at work, or if there were times when he wondered what was going on. For us too, there are times when we cannot see the big picture, and perhaps we wonder what God is doing, but he will always take care of us, if we trust in him.

Drama

Print out short passages of the story, dividing the narrative into smaller chunks, either using an appropriate Bible translation or taking episodes from a children's story Bible. For example:

- Joseph working in Potiphar's house
- Joseph put into prison
- The cupbearer's and the baker's dreams
- Pharaoh's dreams
- Joseph's promotion
- Joseph's family visit Egypt
- Joseph's trick
- The family reunited

Divide the children into smaller groups and ask each group to create a freeze frame, depicting each of these episodes in a single scene. Provide costumes and props as appropriate. Once the children have had time to put their scene together, invite each group to perform their scene as you summarise the story in one narrative.

Talk about the way Joseph served God in each circumstance that he found himself in, both when laid low and when raised high. He did not know how the story would unfold, but he trusted God at every stage.

ICT

Provide safe access to the internet, using either tablets or laptops, and invite the children to research countries presently affected by famine, as Egypt was. If your church has links to a particular charity or ministry, look at the work they do to support those living in famine-affected areas.

Talk about the way that God still cares about those who suffer and what we can do to be like Joseph, who served both God and the people he met who were in difficult circumstances. He was put in a position of great authority, which we do not share, but how can we challenge those who are put in high positions to take better care of the people they are responsible for?

Creative

Source a number of drinking glasses, ideally in a goblet shape, and provide glass paints or pens which the children can use to decorate their own glass with patterns or pictures as they so wish.

Talk about how Joseph was able to interpret the baker's and the cupbearer's dreams and explain what they meant. The cupbearer returned to work in the palace and eventually had the opportunity to save Joseph.

Construction

Provide lolly sticks, scissors and glue and work with the children to create their own miniature storehouse for holding grain. Once the glue has set, you could provide some grain for the children to test out the effectiveness of their structures.

Talk about the reasons why Joseph stored this grain. Children may be familiar with the parable of the rich farmer (Luke 12:16–21) and should be encouraged to explore how these two situations are quite different.

Books

Along with age-appropriate story books about Joseph and children's Bibles, you could also provide a selection of non-fiction books about Ancient Egypt for the children to explore.

Talk about the things that interest the children when they look at the books, as appropriate, and be available to support those less able to read independently.

Prayer and reflective activity

Lay out a large sheet of paper and provide felt pens. Encourage the children to make a note of any of the different ways that God speaks to us, by writing or drawing their ideas.

Talk about the children's and leaders' own experience of God talking to us. Joseph had a gift from God to hear from him through dreams, both his own and other people's. God speaks to us in many different ways.

Games

Set up a relay race, with two large containers of grain at one end of the room, and two empty containers at the opposite end. Divide the children into two teams, and give each team a plastic cup. On the signal to go, players should take turns to use their cup to scoop grain from the first container to transfer to the other. The winning team is the one which transfers the most grain in the time given.

Challenge

Gather a selection of used containers in different shapes and sizes. These could include cardboard boxes, foil food trays, plastic bottles, and so on. You will also need weighing scales and a quantity of grains or cereals. Challenge the children to predict which container will hold the greatest amount of grain, before investigating the result for themselves.

Talk about the way that the people of Egypt were able to store so much grain in the years of plenty, before the famine, that they stopped counting how much there was! What does this tell us about the way we look after our resources?

Prayer

Father God, help us to trust you when times are easy and when times are difficult, just as Joseph and the people of Egypt learned to do. Thank you that you care for us in every circumstance. Amen

Songs

Songs today could include:

- 'Any kind of weather' (Doug Horley)
- 'Brother Joe' (Dave Godfrey)

Take home

This week, you could suggest that the children think about people who are in positions of power, such as Pharaoh and Joseph when he was given a special job to do, and pray for them, that they would make good and wise decisions.

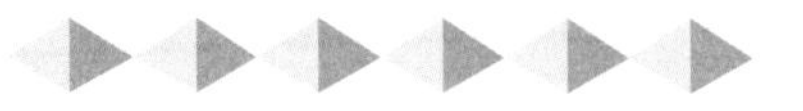

7

The baby in the basket

For the team

Refer to pages 6–9 to see how the activity areas work together

Session theme

This is the first of three sessions which explore some of the key events from the life of Moses. In this session, we discover how God protected Moses as a baby when his life was in danger, and think about what it meant for Moses to be born into such vulnerable circumstances before God raised him to a position of authority.

Bible text: Exodus 2:1–10

Team prayer

Father God, thank you that just as you protected Moses, you have a plan for our lives and will protect us from harm. Amen

Story time

Share the story from a children's Bible story book or from an easy-to-read version of the Bible, perhaps as you prepare for the drama activity, as detailed below.

- How do you feel as you read this story?
- Which character can you relate to most easily, and why?
- What surprised you most about this story?
- Why do you think Moses was kept safe?

Remind the children that we perhaps know this story well and can predict the ending, but Moses' mother did not know how the story would end. She just had to trust God to keep her baby safe from harm. Moses would live a great life, full of adventure, leading God's people to freedom. God protected him from danger at the very beginning of his life.

Say: I wonder if there are times when you, like Moses' mother, cannot see how things will turn out, and wonder about the future. God has his hand on your life, just as he did on Moses', and will work things out for the best for you.

Drama

Set up a hot seat at the front of the group and ask for volunteers to play the part of Moses' mother, his sister and the Egyptian princess. Invite the other children to ask questions of the person sitting in the hot seat, to find out more about their background, what they chose to do and why they acted in the way that they did. Encourage the volunteers to remain in role, supporting them as needed as they think about how their character would respond to the questions asked.

Talk about the different perspectives on the story and how each of the characters acted in the situation they were facing. How does their perspective help us to better understand what happened in the story?

ICT

Provide laptops or tablets with access to the internet and invite the children to search online for information about Ancient Egypt. Encourage the children to think about the themes raised by the story of Moses, the River Nile, the household of the Pharaoh, and the use of slaves to build the great landmarks we still see today.

Talk about the way that finding out more factual information about life in Egypt at this time can help us to better understand the context for the story.

Creative

Provide a range of materials for the children to experiment with weaving. Willow cane is an interesting material to work with on a large scale, or use gardening canes set into a base, with thin sticks to weave between the posts. Small weaving looms can be purchased or made from cardboard to use with wool or ribbon.

Talk about the care that Moses' mother took, preparing the basket ready to hold him. She would not have known how the story would end, but trusted God to keep her baby safe.

Construction

Provide foam or polystyrene blocks and invite the children to help build a pyramid. Encourage them to work together as a group to construct it, thinking about how many blocks they will use on each level to achieve an accurate pyramid shape.

Talk about the way that the slaves in Egypt would have had a very different experience of building pyramids. They would have worked in large groups, simply moving blocks from one point to another, and would have had no say about the process of building the pyramid shapes.

Writing

Provide paper and pens or pencils and invite the children to write a letter, as though they are Moses' mother, which she could have placed in the basket with him. This could be a letter addressed to her son to explain why she has done this, or a 'to whom it may concern' letter, asking the person who finds the baby to take care of her son.

Talk about the way that Moses' mother would have felt as she prepared to leave her son, not knowing if she would ever see him again, but having no other option available to her.

Books

Display a selection of books about Moses and his life, along with children's Bibles. Other books offered today could include a selection of non-fiction books about Ancient Egypt.

Talk about the things that interest the children when they look at the books, as appropriate, and be available to support those less able to read independently.

Prayer and reflective activity

Set out a basket and provide strips of paper and pens. Invite the children to write, on small pieces of paper, the names of people they would like God to look after or protect, before folding the papers up and putting them into the basket.

Talk about the way that God kept Moses safe, and brought him safely to a brand new start. Moses' mother would have prayed that God would keep her baby safe, and he will do the same for the people we care about too.

Games

Divide the children into two teams and give each team a soft doll in a small basket. Ask the children to lie on their backs, with hands in the air, side by side, forming a line from one end of the room to the other. On the signal to start, place the baby and the basket into the hands of the first player of each team. They should then pass the basket from player to player along the line, until it reaches the end of the team. The winning team is the first to get their baby safely to the end of the line.

Prayer

Father God, thank you that you love us and care for us, just as you cared for Moses. Help us to remember that no problem is too great for you to deal with and that you are with us in every circumstance. Amen

Songs

Songs today could include:

- 'Big family of God' (Becky Drake)

Take home

Ask the children if they have any babies or young children in their own or their friends' families. Can they spend some time helping an adult to look after them this week, and think about all the different things they need to do to care for a baby?

8 Escape from Egypt

For the team

Refer to pages 6–9 to see how the activity areas work together

Session theme

This is the second of three sessions exploring the life of Moses. During this session, we will discover more about the plagues that God sent to convince the Pharaoh to set his people free, and about the day when they were finally able to leave Egypt and begin their journey to the promised land. Through this session, we will think about what it means to be set free and how God wants us to be completely free too.

Bible text: Exodus 5—14

Team prayer

Almighty God, thank you for your gift of freedom, which is available to us all. Help us to let go of the things which have no place in our lives, and to accept the freedom you offer. Amen

Story time

This session explores a particularly long story, covering several different episodes. It may work well to partition the story into segments, perhaps retelling some parts orally and looking at other sections in more detail. Alternatively, you could look at different sections of the story in smaller groups, and invite each of them to share their thoughts with the wider group, perhaps as you complete the drama activity, as described below.

- What excites you most about this story?
- What surprises you the most?
- What do we discover about God from this story?
- What do you think you will remember most?

Explain to the children that this is one of the most significant stories in the history of God's people, when we remember how they were set free from their lives as slaves and began a new life. God gave his people another fresh start, a chance to start all over again, full of freedom and promise.

Say: I wonder how we might feel if we were with the Israelites, set free from slavery in Egypt to start all over again. I wonder what things God could set you free from, if you asked him to, so that you could really enjoy being who God wants you to be.

It may be appropriate to follow up some issues raised by this discussion at a later stage.

Drama

Divide the story into several key scenes, perhaps as described below, and ask the children to work in smaller groups, assigning one scene to each, to create a freeze frame, portraying what was happening in each particular element of the story. Scenes used could include:

- Moses and Aaron visit Pharaoh
- Moses hears from God
- Aaron's stick becomes a snake
- The plagues (choose a few if time is limited)
- The Passover
- Pharaoh lets God's people go
- The Israelites cross the Red Sea
- The Egyptians are defeated

You could provide a selection of props and costumes for the children to use, and photograph each of the freeze frames to use to retell the story at a later stage.

Talk about the issues raised by the children as they put their scenes together. How do they think each of the characters felt as the story unfolded? How do they think they would have felt in these different situations?

ICT

Work together with the children to create a stop-motion animation of the crossing of the Red Sea, using play figures to represent the people and blue modelling clay to sculpt the seas as they part. You will also need a laptop with a camera and motion grabbing software to capture the images for the animation.

Talk about how the people must have felt when they reached the Red Sea and discovered they were being chased. How can we capture the magnitude of this episode in our animation sequence?

Creative

Tape up a large strip of lining paper and provide pastels or chalks for the children to use. Encourage the children to help tell the story of the escape from Egypt in the style of Ancient Egyptian wall art. You may find it helpful to have some examples of this style available for the children to use as a stimulus for their own art.

Talk about the way that art can be used to tell a story and discuss the children's ideas for the different images and details that they wish to include.

Construction

Source an old pram wheel chassis and other materials needed for constructing a chariot (similar to a homemade go-kart). Materials might include a large wooden or cardboard box, such as a fruit box, or lengths of wood to construct a standing area. Add relevant extra details and decorate as appropriate.

Talk about the way the Egyptian army chased the Israelites as they made their escape and how they must have felt. They may well have wondered if God was really going to allow them to be free at this stage in the story!

Books

Display the same selection of books as you set out in the previous session, with children's Bibles, a selection of books about Moses and his life, and books about Ancient Egypt.

Talk about the things that interest the children when they look at the books, as appropriate, and be available to support those less able to read independently.

Prayer and reflective activity

Gather a variety of different padlocks with keys, and spread them out on a table. Invite the children to use the keys to try to open each of the padlocks and, as they do so, to think about the different things that God wants to set us free from.

Talk about the way God wanted his people to be free from slavery in Egypt. We are not slaves, but there are things that hold us back too. What does God want to free us from?

Games

Games played today could include those well-known games which involve chasing and catching, such as tag or stuck-in-the-mud, to remind the children of the themes of being caught and set free, as explored in this story.

Challenge

Provide Bibles or children's Bible storybooks, as appropriate to the age of the children. Challenge them to look up and memorise the ten plagues in order, to repeat back when asked at a later stage. They could create a small action to go alongside each plague, to help them to remember them all.

Talk about the reason why God sent the plagues to Egypt, and Pharaoh's stubbornness and refusal to listen to Moses and Aaron. Pharaoh only paid attention when he lost the thing that mattered most to him—his eldest son.

Prayer

Thank you, God, for your gift of freedom. Thank you that you want us to be free to enjoy living as your friends, just as you set the Israelites free from slavery in Egypt. Amen

Songs

Songs today could include:

- 'All through history' (Becky Drake)
- 'No other God' (Paul Jones)

Take home

Challenge the children, when they go home, to find out more about Fairtrade products and to think about those people who are not well cared for by the people who employ them. How do you think God feels about this?

9

God's special rules

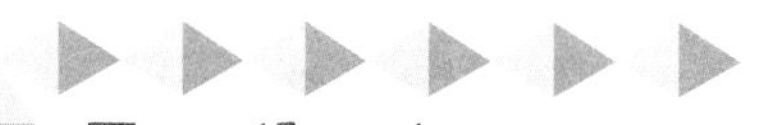

For the team

Refer to pages 6–9 to see how the activity areas work together

Session theme

This is the final session in a series of three, exploring some of the events from the life of Moses. We will explore God's special rules, the ten commandments, and why they are as important today as they were to the Israelites when they were first given to them by God.

Bible text: Exodus 19—20

Team prayer

Father God, thank you that you want the best for us, and that you gave us these rules to teach us the best way to live. Help us to share these rules with the children we work with and to communicate your heart for all your people, as children loved by you. Amen

Story time

As you begin this story time, explain the context to the children—how God's people had been released from their lives as slaves in Egypt, but still were not happy and could not settle into a new way of life which pleased God. Explain that this is why God gave his people the ten commandments. Use an appropriate translation of the Bible to look at the text of Exodus 20:1–20, perhaps printing out copies of the passage so that the children can annotate the text as you discuss it.

- Do any of these rules surprise you?
- What special rules do you think God's people should follow?
- Are there any rules that you would add or take away?
- Why do you think God gave these rules to the people?

Discuss the issues and ideas raised by the children, and share how Jesus later explained the ten commandments in more detail (Matthew 5:17–48), reminding us that how we feel and think about people is as important as the actions we actually take.

Say: I wonder how many of these rules are easy to follow. I wonder which ones you find more difficult. When we remember what Jesus said, we set the bar higher. To do this we must remember what it really means to love God and love other people, just as God asks us to.

Drama

Provide copies of the ten commandments or Bibles for the children to look up the text themselves, and divide the children into smaller groups. Ask each small group to choose one of the commandments and create a short sketch which demonstrates what their selected commandment means and how we can put it into action in our daily lives.

Talk about what the children understand their chosen commandment to mean and how we live it out day by day. Are there any commandments which we may find more challenging to follow than others?

ICT

Provide a tablet with a Bible app installed, or a laptop with access to the internet so that the children can search through different translations of the Bible. Invite them to look at today's passage in different translations to find the commandments explained in different ways. You could invite the children to print or write out some of the different wordings that help them to understand the rules better.

Talk about the way that all our Bibles are translated from the original text. Sometimes we cannot find a perfect translation and so words can be interpreted in different ways. Sometimes words we use change over time, so it helps to look at different ways of explaining a text to better understand what God is saying.

Construction

Use chicken wire to form a frame of a mountainous landscape and invite the children to cover the basic form with Modroc or papier mâché to create a mountain construction.

Talk about the fact that we have direct access to God, which people at the time of this story did not. God revealed himself to Moses and the Israelites when Moses had climbed up Mount Sinai, and there God spoke to Moses about the way his people should behave and act. This was an incredible encounter for Moses.

Writing

Provide a wide selection of writing tools and surfaces, with which the children can experiment. These could include clay and clay-working tools, leather and appropriate tools, slates and chalk, parchment, different papers and cards and a selection of pens, pencils, paintbrushes and quills.

Talk about the way that God provided the ten commandments written on two slabs of stone, to indicate the agreement between God and his people that they would follow his rules.

Books

Present the books about Moses and his lifetime, along with the children's Bible that you used for the previous sessions. You could also source some leaflets about safety, such as those about the Green Cross Code.

Talk about the things that interest the children when they look at the books, as appropriate, and be available to support those less able to read independently. Talk about the leaflets provided and how rules exist for our safety. God set his rules in place to keep his people safe.

Prayer and reflective activity

Print out copies of each of God's ten special rules, each on a separate strip of paper. Provide two larger paper hearts with Jesus' two commandments written on them, 'Love God' on one heart and 'Love others' on the other (see Matthew 22:37–40). Help the children to sort the ten commandments into those two sets: 'Love God' and 'Love others'.

Talk about the fact that Jesus gave us these two rules not to say that the ten commandments don't matter, but rather to say that if we love God and other people, we will naturally keep the ten commandments.

Games

Set up some well-known team games, such as simple versions of football or basketball but without any rules. Stand and watch as the children start to play the game, but do not umpire; just let the children see how things begin to go wrong when there are no rules to follow.

Prayer

Father God, thank you that you want the best for all of us, to keep us safe and to make sure that we care for one another. We are sorry for the times when we don't live in the way that we should. Help us to remember to love you and to love others, just as you commanded. Amen

Songs

Songs today could include:

- '10 rules, 1 God' (Dave Godfrey)
- 'If I've been wrong' (Sammy Horner)

Take home

Provide copies of the hearts with the words 'Love God' and 'Love others' written on them, as used for the prayer and reflective activity, for the children to take home with them. Encourage them to display the hearts somewhere as a reminder that all the decisions we make should come from these two commandments.

10

Joshua and the walls of Jericho

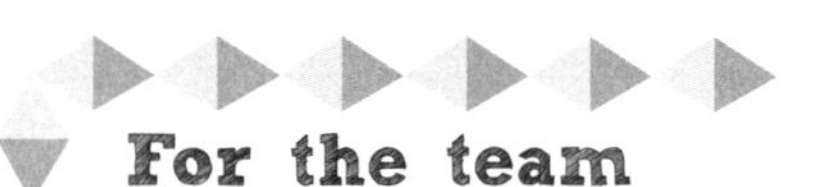

For the team

Refer to pages 6–9 to see how the activity areas work together

Session theme

This session explores one of the episodes in the story of the Israelites on their journey towards the promised land. We will discover what it meant for God's people to follow his instructions, even when those instructions seemed strange, and so enter the city, as he had promised they would.

Bible text: Joshua 6

Team prayer

Father God, help us to trust you and follow your instructions, no matter how unlikely they seem, just as the Israelites did when entering the city of Jericho. Amen

Story time

Use an age-appropriate translation of the Bible to look at the story, or refer to the text as you complete the drama activity and think about the discussion points raised below.

- What do you find surprising about this story?
- How do you think Joshua would have felt as these events took place?
- How do you think you would have felt if you had been there?
- What do we discover about God from this story?

Explain to the children that God's people had already been through a number of difficult situations since they left Egypt. Sometimes they trusted God willingly and other times they found it hard to believe what God said to them. In this story, God gave Joshua some pretty unlikely instructions to follow, but Joshua trusted God, and did exactly as he said. He could then enter the city of Jericho, just as God promised.

Say: I wonder if there are times when it seems difficult to follow God's instructions, or when it's hard to trust the things that he says. God can always be trusted. He will never let us down when we do things his way.

Activity areas

Drama

Provide a selection of simple props, such as trumpets (perhaps created from rolled-up paper), armour, the ark, and perhaps cardboard box walls. Assign roles to the children and explain that as you read the text of the story, they should improvise and act out what happened, listening carefully to the details as you read. Take time over the retelling, explaining any elements to the children as necessary, and encouraging them to act out the story appropriately.

Talk about the things that the children notice about the story as they act out each part. What do they find surprising? How do they think they would have felt if they had been there when it happened?

ICT

Provide laptops or tablets and access to the internet and invite the children to find Jericho on a map in order to place it in relation to some of the other places they have already heard about (Egypt, Canaan, Mount Sinai, and so on), as well as places that are known to them today.

Talk about the way that God's people spent many, many years travelling around this area because they were not ready to enter the promised land. What do we know about this part of the world today? How can we pray for this region?

Creative

Provide images of the ark of the covenant, along with cardboard boxes, gold paint, paintbrushes, scissors and other craft materials, and invite the children to work together to create a model of the ark of the covenant, which can be used in a dramatic retelling of the story.

Talk about what the ark of the covenant contained and why it was so significant to God's people. Explain how it was used in today's story, as the priests marched around the city walls, and why the people had to follow God's instructions.

Construction

Provide small building bricks or blocks for the children to use to build a detailed model of the city walls. You could help to inspire them by displaying some photographs of castles or other ancient walled cities.

Talk about the way that communities built city walls around them to protect them from enemies, but that nothing could stand in God's way.

Books

Provide a selection of children's Bibles and age-appropriate books including the story of Joshua and other stories about the time God's people spent trying to reach the promised land. You could also provide a selection of atlases in which children can find the places mentioned in these stories.

Talk about the stories that children are familiar with from this period, and the reasons why God's people were unable to enter the promised land immediately. Support children with reading as necessary.

Prayer and reflective activity

Gather a selection of pebbles and invite the children to work with you to build a number of pebble towers or sculptures at different heights.

Talk about how there are times to build things up and times to tear things down (Ecclesiastes 3:3b). What things does God want us to build up? What things does he want to tear down, like the walls of Jericho?

Games

Games offered today could include Jenga or other building or balancing games. A Giant Jenga game would work well with a large group of children, if space allows.

Prayer

Almighty God, thank you that no problem is too big or too difficult for you. Help us to trust you, as Joshua and his army did, and to do the things you say. Amen

Songs

Songs today could include:

- 'Joshua fought the battle of Jericho' (Traditional)
- 'Nothing's too big, big, big for his power' (Doug Horley)

Take home

Invite the children to take a pebble away with them from the prayer and reflective activity as a reminder of this story, and to think about whether there may be things in their own lives which God wants to build up or tear down.

11
Ruth: someone who cared

For the team

Refer to pages 6–9 to see how the activity areas work together

Session theme

This session tells the story of how Ruth cared for Naomi and how, in turn, Boaz cared for Ruth. We will consider how families of all shapes and sizes care for one another and how we can welcome and include others in our own families.

Bible text: Ruth 1—4

Team prayer

Father God, thank you for those who have cared for us and modelled what it means to be a welcoming family. Help us to welcome and accept others into our group, and to show what it means for us to love and care for them. Amen

Story time

Today's story is made up of a number of separate episodes, told in sequence. You may choose to retell some of these verbally, and look together at others in a Bible or children's story Bible, or you may choose to divide the story into different sections which smaller groups of children can take a look at, before sharing what they have discovered with one another, when you regroup.

- How does this story make you feel?
- Who can you most relate to in this story and why?
- How did the different characters honour God in the way they acted?
- What do you think happens when we care for one another in this way?

Remind the children that each of the characters had choices to make at different points in the story. The decisions that they made were unlikely to have been the easiest decisions, and in every case they thought about the needs of other people before taking care of themselves. Ruth put Naomi first, Naomi put Ruth first and Boaz took care of them both.

Say: I wonder what opportunities we have to put other people before ourselves. Perhaps these decisions are easy to make, or perhaps we have to give up something for ourselves in order to make sure that the other person has what they need. How different do you think the world would be if we all put other people's needs first? How do you think God would feel about this?

Drama

Prepare a number of different cards, giving details of different situations where people can show how to care for one another. These could include a parent and child, a nurse and patient or a teacher and pupil. Ask the children to create a short drama sketch to show how their given characters care for one another.

Talk about the ideas the children have about how each of these characters care for one another, and how we can show that care through the scenarios they act out.

ICT

Offer a word processing programme with word art facilities for the children to use to create a simple family tree, using text boxes and lines to link the boxes as appropriate. Alternatively, you can download simple family tree programmes online, which they can use to enter their family information, or that of a fictitious family, if they prefer.

Talk about the way that the different generations of our families are connected and how they take care of one another. How do we care for our own family, as Ruth cared for hers?

Creative

Working with the children, follow a simple recipe to make a loaf of bread together (perhaps using a quick bread recipe). If you have no baking facilities, you could offer a taste test activity, using different types of bread for the children to compare. (Remember to check for allergies.)

Talk about the way that grains grown in the field are still a staple ingredient of our diet today. Boaz made sure that he did what he could to provide the things that Ruth and Naomi would need to survive in difficult times.

Construction

Gather a supply of cardboard boxes and invite the children to construct model houses, perhaps providing dolls and doll's house furniture to place into them, or asking the children to create their own.

Talk about the way that Ruth wanted to create a home for Naomi and how Boaz, in turn, wanted to welcome them into his home. What makes our homes feel special to us? Why is the idea of home so well linked to the idea of family?

Writing

Provide a selection of thank-you cards or craft materials for the children to make their own, as well as envelopes and pens, and invite them to write a thank-you card to someone who cares for them. This could be a childminder or teacher, or perhaps someone who works for the emergency services.

Talk about the many different people who care for us in different ways. Naomi would have had nobody to look after her if Ruth hadn't chosen to stay with her.

Books

Alongside children's Bibles and story books retelling the story of Ruth and Naomi, you could also provide a selection of age-appropriate children's story books which explore the theme of family and different family groupings today.

Share the books with the children, supporting any children who need help with reading. Discuss the issues raised by these books, particularly around the theme of family and what it means to belong to a family.

Prayer and reflective activity

Set out a large sheet of paper and invite the children to help you to create a poster titled 'Our big family'. This could include members of the children's group you are running, as well as the wider church family, as appropriate. You could invite the children to draw or paint the different people on to the poster, or take digital photographs (with permission of parents or carers) to print out and stick on to the paper provided.

Talk about what it means to belong to a family, whether or not you are blood relatives. How can we welcome people into our family? How can we care for one another, as Ruth cared for Naomi?

Games

Prepare a number of sticky labels with different names of members of well-known families on each, ensuring that each family group has the same number of members. Stick one label on to the back of each player. On the signal to begin, ask the children to go around and ask the other players questions which can only have a yes or no answer, to find out their identity before finding the other members of their family groups.

Prayer

Father God, thank you that we are all members of your great big family. Help us to show love to others, welcoming them into your family, just as Ruth showed love to Naomi. Amen

Songs

Songs today could include:

- 'You can reach out with a heart of love' (Doug Horley)

Take home

Challenge the children to think about different ways their own families can show love and care to other people, planning to do something special with their parents. This may involve inviting a friend round for dinner or baking a cake for a neighbour, for instance.

12

Samuel: a boy who listened

For the team

Refer to pages 6–9 to see how the activity areas work together

Session theme

This session retells the story of how God first spoke to Samuel as a young boy and explores how we can all hear from God today, regardless of age, status or experience. This session offers some practical ideas for how you can create space for the children to listen to God, both within the activities of the group, and also when they leave and go home.

Bible text: 1 Samuel 3

Team prayer

Help us, Father God, to have ears open to hear from you and hearts ready to respond to the things that you say. Help us to create space for the children we work with, so that they may hear from you too and build their own relationships with you. Amen

Story time

Today's story can be explored in more detail as you prepare the drama activity. Alternatively, take some time to read the story together from the Bible, or from a children's story Bible, as a separate activity.

- What surprises you about this story?
- How do you think you would have responded if you were Samuel?
- How do you think you would have responded if you were Eli?
- What do we discover about God from this story?

Explain to the children that, at this time in God's story, it was unusual for people to hear directly from God and only certain people were granted this privilege, as Samuel was. This was the first of many times that God would speak to Samuel who would later share messages from God with many people, following God's instructions. What was even more unusual was that Samuel was only a young boy and yet God still chose to speak to him.

Say: I wonder if anyone here has already heard God speak to them. I wonder if we know how we can tell that God is speaking to us. Today, God speaks to all those who follow him, in many different ways. We are going to explore some of these different ideas today, and we would love to help you to explore what this means for you.

Drama

Provide Bibles, Bible story books, or printouts of the story, and work together with the children to create a radio drama of the story, using props to create sound effects and voices to tell the story in the first person. Once the children have had time to construct and rehearse, record their drama using appropriate audio equipment.

Talk about the children's ideas for how they can retell the story, using only sounds, and how important it was for Samuel to listen to God.

ICT

Provide secure access to the internet on laptops or tablets to find images of the tabernacle at Shiloh, as it would have looked at the time of Samuel and Eli. If appropriate, the children could print a selection of images to help with the construction activity.

Talk about the different features of the tabernacle, why it was so important and what it represented to God's people.

Creative

Provide some simple notebooks, along with a selection of decorative papers, ribbons, stickers, pens and glue. Invite the children to use the materials provided to create their own prayer journal, decorating the cover as they wish and jotting down some ideas on the first page about how they want to use their journal.

Talk about how they can use a prayer journal, perhaps making a note of the things that they pray for, and what happens when they pray. Encourage the children to bring their journals back from time to time to share how they are being used.

Construction

Offer a wide selection of junk modelling items in different shapes and sizes, made from different materials, which the children can use to create an accurate and detailed model of the tabernacle as it would have been at the time of Samuel. You could also provide post-it notes and pens for the children to label the key features.

Talk about how each aspect of the tabernacle would have been important and the role it played for God's people then. Do our church buildings hold the same importance for us today?

Writing

Prepare small pieces of paper in a range of colours, perhaps cut into question mark shapes, and invite the children to write their own questions to God on each piece of paper, before sticking them up to create a 'Questions for God' display board.

Talk about each of the questions that the children write down, perhaps helping them to find answers as appropriate, without oversimplifying more complex ideas. Help the children to think about how we may find answers to more difficult questions and how sometimes there are things that may be too difficult for us to understand.

Prayer and reflective activity

Create a quiet zone, maybe under a gazebo or similar structure. This could be furnished with soft cushions, battery-operated candles or coloured lights, Bibles, paper and pens.

Talk about how this area can be used and encourage the children to remain quiet in it. If the children want to talk about anything as a result of being in this quiet space, encourage them to do so in another part of the room.

Games

Prepare some recordings of well-known television programme theme tunes, and provide paper and pens. Ask the children to work in small groups to listen to each of the tracks, and write down which television show they think each tune is from. You could award a small prize to the winning team.

Prayer

Father God, thank you that we can talk to you about anything. Help us to remember that you talk to us too, and help us to be ready to listen to the things you say, just as Samuel did. Amen

Songs

Songs today could include:

- 'You need to natter to God' (Doug Horley)
- 'Your eyes' (David Wakerly, Beci Wakerly and Julia A'Bell)

Take home

Encourage the children to take their prayer journals home with them and to start using them in the coming week. You could invite the group to bring their journals back with them next week to talk about the way they are using them, and the way that God answers prayer.

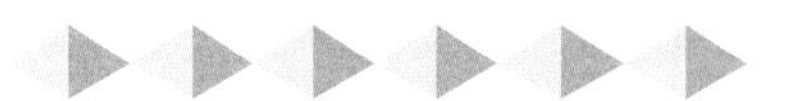

13

David and Goliath

For the team

Refer to pages 6–9 to see how the activity areas work together

Session theme

In this session, we discover how a young boy's unwavering trust in God enabled God's people to defeat their enemy. This is the first of three sessions exploring some of the episodes from the life of David, and what we can learn from the example that he set.

Bible text: 1 Samuel 17

Team prayer

Father God, there are times, even as adults, when we feel small or insignificant. Help us to have faith like a child, and to trust you in every circumstance, remembering that nothing is too difficult for you. Amen

Story time

As you begin this session, you may wish to unpick the story as you prepare the drama activity, or as a separate discussion, taking some time to look at the story in a Bible or children's story Bible.

- How does this story make you feel?
- Who surprises you most?
- How do you think you would have responded if you were David?
- Why do you think he was so confident when he approached Goliath?

Help the children to understand that David had absolute confidence that God would enable him to defeat Goliath, because he had total trust in God and all he said and did. The rest of Saul's army were thinking about things they were, or were not, capable of, and doubted they would be able to defeat the giant. They had forgotten the way that God would look after them.

Say: I wonder if there are big problems we face, like David. Do we try to fix these problems on our own, or do we trust God to help us? No matter how small or insignificant we may feel, God can and will enable us to do great things for him, when we stop relying on ourselves.

Drama

Provide Bibles, children's story Bibles or copies of the text and work together with the children to act out what happened in the story. You could ask the shortest child to play the part of David, and the tallest leader to play Goliath, and provide a selection of appropriate costumes and props for the children to use in their dramatic retelling.

Talk about the ideas the children have for retelling the story, which important details to include and how to portray the events of the story.

ICT

Provide laptops or tablets and access to the internet and invite the children to research how tall Goliath actually was, before comparing this to record-holding tallest men and women in the world today.

Talk about how everyone was intimidated by Goliath, and understandably so. Why do you think David felt so brave?

Creative

Gather a selection of small, smooth pebbles and provide acrylic paints and paintbrushes. Invite the children to paint a picture or pattern on the pebble, or perhaps write a message, which reminds them of the story.

Talk about how David was able to defeat Goliath with just one small pebble. Ask the children what we want to remember from this story.

Construction

Collect a supply of old newspapers and give them to the children, with a roll of masking tape. Challenge the children to work together to construct the tallest free-standing tower they can, using only the newspaper and masking tape. They could all work together to complete the challenge or work in competing teams to see which team can construct the best tower.

Talk about how unsteady the newspaper towers became, the taller you built them. Goliath, although also tall, certainly wasn't unsteady, and Saul's army were finding it very hard to defeat him. David trusted God to help him, and he managed to topple Goliath with one blow.

Books

Provide a selection of children's Bibles which retell this and other stories from the life of David, for the children to look at and read. You could also offer a selection of biographies about other children or young people, telling how they served God.

Share the books with the children, supporting them with their reading as appropriate, and talking about the things that interest them.

Prayer and reflective activity

Lay out a selection of newspapers and invite the children to pull out the stories of situations which make us feel intimidated or small. Perhaps these will be some of the world news stories which are far removed from us, or situations which feel too overwhelming to begin to address.

Talk about how we can begin to pray for some of these situations that seem beyond us, in the knowledge that nothing is too big or difficult for God to deal with.

Games

Provide a selection of target games or catapulting games, under appropriate supervision. These could include a magnetic dartboard, a basketball or netball hoop, or games with water pistols and targets. David would have been a good shot after the time he spent protecting the sheep, using this skill to defeat Goliath in one blow.

Prayer

Father God, thank you that no matter how small we may feel, there is nothing that we face that is too big or too difficult for you to deal with. Help us to trust you no matter what we are facing, just as David did. Amen

Songs

Songs today could include:

- 'Have we made our God too small?' (Doug Horley)
- 'Nothing's too big' (Doug Horley)

Take home

Encourage the children to take some time to think about any difficult problems they may be facing, perhaps writing them down on a piece of paper, and to remember that God is bigger than all our problems or worries. Suggest that they may want to share these things with an adult they trust, as they pray that God would help them.

David and Jonathan

Refer to pages 6–9 to see how the activity areas work together

For the team

Session theme

This is the second of three sessions which explore the life of David. In this session, we celebrate the friendship of David and Jonathan, remembering the courageous way that David and Jonathan acted, putting God's will first, even when it was difficult.

Bible text: 1 Samuel 18—20

Team prayer

Father God, thank you for the example of Jonathan, who worked hard to protect his friend, and David, who chose not to harm Saul, even when given the opportunity. Sometimes, it can be difficult to stand up as your followers; help us to walk in your way continually, even when it is difficult. Amen

Story time

Today's story ranges over a long series of episodes involving David and Jonathan. You may wish to select some key events in the story to look at together, either working as a whole group or assigning short passages to smaller groups to explore, ready to feed back to the wider group. You could combine this with the drama activity or include it in a separate story time.

- What did you enjoy about this story?
- How did Jonathan act as a good friend to David?
- How did David act as a good friend to Jonathan?
- What challenges you about this story?

Explain to the group that both David and Jonathan showed immense bravery in the way they acted. Jonathan chose to disobey his father repeatedly, because he knew it was the right thing to do. David also made difficult decisions to do the right thing, choosing not to harm Saul, even though he was given many opportunities, because he knew it would be wrong. Both David and Jonathan put God first and helped each other to grow as followers of God.

Say: I wonder how our friends help us to grow as followers of God. I wonder what we do to help our friends to grow too. We may not be running away from a dangerous and powerful king, but we all face difficult situations from time to time and can help those around us to face those problems and deal with them in the best way possible.

Activity areas

Drama

Select some key episodes from the story about the friendship between David and Jonathan. Divide the children into smaller groups and give each group a different piece of the story to portray dramatically, perhaps providing printouts of each section of the story, or dividing up the text from a children's Bible, as appropriate. You could also provide a selection of appropriate costumes and props for the children to use. After they have had time to rehearse their scenes, ask each group to perform their scene in order, retelling the whole story to one another.

Talk about the issues raised in each of the scenes, as the children create their part of the drama, and any questions or ideas that they may have, as you complete this activity.

ICT

Set up a photo booth, with a selection of fancy dress costumes and various props. Invite the children to dress up and pose for a photo within friendship groups of their choosing, being careful to ensure that nobody is left out, before printing copies for them to take away.

Talk about the things we enjoy doing with our friends and how our friendships develop when we have fun together. David and Jonathan's friendship was tested in the midst of difficult circumstances.

Creative

Source an unwanted old chair and provide a selection of materials which can be used to upcycle the chair to create a throne. Materials required may include paints, perhaps metallic, and different fabrics along with the appropriate glues and scissors. You could provide some photos of thrones to inspire the children in their creativity.

Talk about how David joined the royal household knowing that God had chosen him to one day become king. He continued to respect Saul as king, even when he made bad choices and tried to hurt David.

Construction

Work together with the children to construct a model cave, perhaps on a large scale, using chicken wire to create a frame before covering it in Modroc or papier mâché, or smaller model caves from clay.

Talk about the way that Jonathan helped his friend to escape, putting his own life at risk and helping him to hide out in caves.

Writing

Provide a selection of notecards or materials to make simple notecards, and invite the children to write a card to one of their friends to thank them for their friendship, to let them know why they are special to them or to encourage them.

Talk about why friendships matter to us. God designed us to live in community with other people and to have relationships. How can we support, love and encourage our friends?

Books

Books provided today should include children's Bibles and a selection of age-appropriate story books about the life of David.

Share the books with the children, supporting them with reading as necessary and helping them to discover more about David and the part he played in God's story.

Prayer and reflective activity

Provide paper, pencils, paint and brushes and invite the children to work with you to create a portrait of David and Jonathan, in appropriate clothing for the time.

Talk about each of the men and the way they chose to do the right thing, even when it was difficult. David had the opportunity to hurt Saul, but chose not to because he knew it would not have been what God wanted, and Jonathan often stood up to Saul in order to protect his friend. Talk about the difficult situations that the children find themselves in, while trying to follow God.

Games

Prepare a set of sticky labels with the names of famous pairings written on them (one name per card) such as Ant and Dec, Batman and Robin, Mickey and Minnie Mouse. Stick one label on to each child's back and invite them to try to find their partner, by first asking questions which can only have yes or no as an answer, to find out who they are.

Talk about how David and Jonathan have become well known for their friendship, as these other characters have too.

Prayer

Father God, thank you for our friends, for those people who help us to do the right thing, and the people that we can talk to about you, helping us both to grow as your followers. Help us to be good friends, like David and Jonathan, putting other people first and respecting other people in the way that you would want us to. Amen

Songs

Songs today could include:

- 'Never give up' (Brittany Grey)

Take home

Suggest that the children do one special thing for a friend this week, to let them know how much they value their friendship.

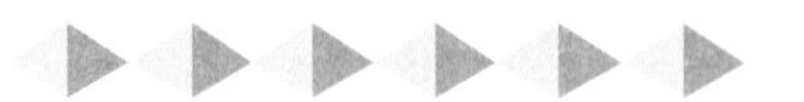

15

King David praises God

For the team

Refer to pages 6–9 to see how the activity areas work together

Session theme

This is the third and final session exploring some key events from the life of David. In this session, we discover more about the way that David worshipped God, through song and dance, and his hopes and dreams to build the temple. It was God's will that his son Solomon would complete the work, but through this session, we discover more about how we can follow David's example and live as people who put God first.

Bible text: 1 Chronicles 17 and 22—29

Team prayer

Almighty God, you are a great God, who should have first place in our lives at all times. Help us to worship you as David did, through prayer and song, dancing and arts, and above all, through the way we live our daily lives. Amen

Story time

This story is made up of several small episodes. A leader could retell the whole story to the children for them to discuss, as appropriate. Alternatively, it may work well to divide the children into smaller groups and assign a short part of the Bible text to each group to look at together, with adult support. Ask each small group to look at what happens in their own part of the story before retelling it to the wider group.

- What did you find interesting about this story?
- What did you find surprising?
- What motivated David to do these things?
- What do we discover about God from this story?

Explain that when we speak of worshipping God, we often limit ourselves to talking about the songs we might sing, perhaps in church. Worship is about giving God the whole of our lives, because we want to show him what he means to us. David had been through many highs and lows in his life and he had learned what it meant to show God how precious he was to him, which is why he praised God in many different ways.

Say: I wonder how we choose to praise God. I wonder if we find it easy to relate to the way David felt about God, or whether it is something we feel we want to understand more. Remind the children that you are there to help them explore and grow their relationship with God and that you would love to help them as they discover more about what it means to praise God for who he is to them.

Drama

Provide Bibles or printouts of a selection of psalms written by David.

These could include:

- Psalm 8
- Psalm 19
- Psalm 24
- Psalm 63

Invite the children to select a psalm to use for this activity and then create a mime to interpret the words of the psalm as it is read to them. Larger groups could be divided into smaller groups to create a number of different mimes, which can be performed to one another after they have had time to rehearse.

Talk about the children's ideas for interpreting the words of the psalms. How can we praise God through our words? How can we praise God in our physical actions?

ICT

Provide laptops or tablets with access to the internet and invite the children to research Solomon's temple and find out more about the temple that was eventually built, after David's death.

Talk about how this building would have stood out at the time as the only building of its type and scale. How does this building compare to our cathedrals and churches? Do you think David could have imagined what would eventually be built, when he first began the process?

Creative

Ask one of your leaders to prepare a short dance routine that can be taught to any interested children. This could include the use of ribbons or streamers, or include actions or sign language as appropriate to the children in your group.

Talk about how some people use music and dance to help them express their worship to God, just as David did. Talk about the different ideas raised by the particular piece of music that you choose to use for this activity.

Construction

Provide a selection of junk modelling and collage materials that the children can use to design their own temple or special building for God. Show photographs of some of our large historic cathedrals, as well as pictures of the temple which Solomon built, to show how people have expressed their worship of God through design and architecture.

Talk about how God no longer needs to dwell in a temple, but we can still express our worship to God through creativity and design.

Writing

Print out copies of some of David's psalms of praise and invite the children to write their own. They could write their own psalms independently, or simply write a line or two on a strip of paper which could then be collated together to create a group psalm to use together in your prayer time.

Talk about the children's ideas as they record them, and about how we can use words to express our worship to God.

Books

Set out the books used in the previous sessions, retelling some of the stories from the life of David, as well as children's Bibles.

Talk about the things that interest the children when they look at the books, as appropriate, and be available to support those less able to read independently.

Prayer and reflective activity

Provide copies of more of David's psalms of praise, or a children's book of psalms for the children to read. Depending upon the psalms chosen, this may be a quiet reflective time or a noisy musical praise session, so additional resources may be required.

Talk about the way that David's psalms were one expression of his worship of God that we use today and how his words still carry meaning for us, so many years after he first wrote them.

Games

Set up a treasure hunt, for the children to search for a specific list of items, either in the room where you meet, or in the local area. This could be done in a number of different ways, following a set of clues, collecting together different objects, or even photographing the things you ask them to find.

Talk about how David sent out a list of building materials that they would need to build the temple and involved people in finding the materials.

Prayer

Father God, thank you that we can worship you and show how much you mean to us, in many different ways. Help us to put you first, every day that we live, and to worship you in every aspect of our lives. Amen

Songs

Songs today could include:

- 'Find a way (to give you praise)' (Mark Depledge)
- 'I can't run enough' (Dave Godfrey)

Take home

Print out a few more of David's psalms and encourage the children to look at them this week. Suggest that they read these psalms when they are talking to God at home. How can they help us to worship God?

16
Elijah and the fire

For the team

Refer to pages 6–9 to see how the activity areas work together

Session theme

In this session, we discover one of the stories about the prophet Elijah and how he challenged King Ahab in his beliefs. As a messenger of God, Elijah was not afraid to share God's messages with people, no matter how challenging or difficult. This session reminds us that our God is able to deal with all challenges; nothing is too difficult for him.

Bible text: 1 Kings 18

Team prayer

Thank you, God, that you are the true God, who will never let us down. You are in every circumstance and every situation, and nothing is too difficult for you. Amen

Story time

Share the story together, looking at the Bible passage, or in a children's Bible story book, or perhaps retelling the story orally. Alternatively, discuss the points and questions suggested below as you complete the drama activity.

- How do you think Elijah felt when he stood on the mountain?
- What do you think King Ahab and his men expected to happen?
- What surprised you most about this story?
- What do we discover about God?

Explain to the children that this story happened during a difficult period for God's people, when they had a series of different rulers, some who were good and others who had their own ideas about how to govern the people, not following God's instructions. There were many times when God's people found it hard to trust God and to do the things that he said, but through all of this God was faithful to his people and never let them down.

Say: I wonder if there are times when we find it hard to trust God. I wonder if there are times when we feel as though we are on our own in trusting God. Just as God was there for Elijah, he is there for us too. We are never on our own when we follow God; he is always with us.

Activity areas

Drama

Ask for one volunteer to play the part of Elijah and the other children to stand on the side of Ahab. Provide a selection of props, including stones (or small boxes) for building the altars, a watering can and coloured cellophane or tissue paper flames. As you read the story, encourage the children to ad lib appropriately, playing the roles they have been assigned, and responding to the story as their given characters would.

Talk about how surprising this story was. When the story begins and you see Elijah standing alone, you may wonder what he could do against the king and all his men, but Elijah had God on his side and was not alone.

ICT

Set up a laptop with a camera and simple motion grabbing software to create a short stop motion animation film which retells the story of Elijah and how God sent fire on the altar. You will need small play figures for the characters and simple props such as stones to build the altar and fiery coloured modelling clay or cellophane to represent the flames.

Talk about how the children will retell the story, perhaps sketching a simple storyboard first, as they think about how to include all the details needed.

Creative

Source a number of plain glass tea-light holders, together with tissue paper in fiery colours and PVA glue, or glass paints or pens. Invite the children to decorate their own tea-light holder to create a flame design around the glass. You could provide a tea-light or battery operated tea-light for the children to put into their holder to see the decoration light up.

Talk about the way that God sent fire down to the altar, consuming everything that was there and proving that he is the one true God.

Construction

Provide copies of the passage 1 Kings 18:30–35 and access to the things that the children will need to build the altar in the same way that Elijah did: large stones, wood and water, perhaps in a sand tray where they can dig a trench too. Invite the children to read the passage and to copy the actions of Elijah in building his altar.

Talk about each element of the altar, what the stones represented, why Elijah poured water over it, and so on. Explain that in Elijah's time, people had to make sacrifices to God for the things they had done wrong, but when Jesus went to the cross, that was the ultimate sacrifice, made for each of us.

Writing

Provide some flame shapes cut from red, orange and yellow paper and invite the children to write their own prayers on these flames, which can later be combined with the rock shapes used in the prayer and reflective activity, to create a small display.

Talk about how the children feel about praying independently, and any issues or questions raised. This story reminds us that God is the true God who hears and answers our prayers.

Books

Display a selection of children's Bibles and Bible story books, retelling this and other stories from the life of Elijah.

Talk about the things that interest the children when they look at the books, as appropriate, and be available to support those less able to read independently. You may like to explain more about who Elijah was, and the things that he did.

Prayer and reflective activity

Prepare some cards in rock shapes and invite the children to add their own names for God, or words to describe God on each of the paper rocks. Use the shapes to build a picture of the altar.

Talk about the way that altars were used at this time to make a sacrifice to God as an act of worship. We do not need to do this any more as we use other ways of telling God how great he is.

Prayer

Father God, thank you that you are the true God and that nothing is too big or too difficult for you. Help us to trust in you, just as Elijah did, and do the things that you say. Amen

Songs

Songs today could include:

- 'No other God' (Paul Jones)

Take home

Challenge the children when they go home to discover more of the stories of Elijah, perhaps using a Bible or children's Bible story book, or using an online Bible. If appropriate, you may wish to provide them with a list of particular passages to look up, to discover more about this messenger of God.

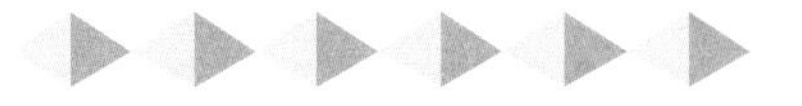

17 Daniel and the lions

For the team

Refer to pages 6–9 to see how the activity areas work together

Session theme

This story is one which many children may remember from early childhood, if only for the lions which did not eat Daniel. In this session, we explore the bravery of a man who chose to continue to worship God, even though he knew he was putting his life at risk, because he knew that nothing was more precious than his relationship with God. There is also an opportunity to discover a little more about the persecuted church—those who still put themselves at great risk for their faith in God.

Bible text: Daniel 6

Team prayer

Father God, thank you for the freedom we enjoy to live openly as your followers. Help us, this day, to take courage when we are facing difficult situations, knowing that nothing is more precious to us than you. Amen

Story time

Share today's story, either by looking at an appropriate Bible translation or story book together, or by retelling the story orally.

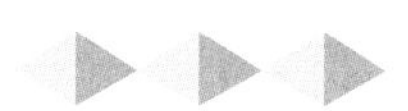

- How does this story make you feel?
- What surprises you most?
- How are we challenged by this story?
- What do we discover about God?

Explain to the children that Daniel knew he was putting his life at risk by continuing to pray to God and disobeying the orders that had been put in place, but that his relationship with God mattered more, and he would not break God's special rule by worshipping another god. God protected Daniel when he sent the angel to close the mouths of the lions. When other people saw what God had done, they too chose to put him first.

Say: I wonder if there are times when you find it hard to put God first. I wonder whether we would be able to put God first, as Daniel did when things became really difficult. All around the world, many people face times when it is difficult to follow God and sometimes terrible things happen to these people. The Bible reminds us that no matter what we go through here on earth, God will be here with us.

Drama

Prepare a number of different scenarios, writing them out on smaller cards before the session, around situations where the children may find it difficult to live openly as a Christian. These could include, among others:

- When they are being teased for going to church.
- When something terrible happens and people ask, 'How can God let this happen?'
- A topic being explored at school seems to make things you read about in the Bible more difficult to believe.

Invite the children to prepare a short sketch, showing how they could respond in these circumstances.

Talk about the way that sometimes it can be difficult to acknowledge openly that you are a Christian or that you believe in God. The Bible tells us that we will face difficult or testing situations. Sometimes it can be really helpful to think about different ways we could respond, before we find ourselves put on the spot. God will be with us, just as he was with Daniel, and will help us to deal with these challenges.

ICT

Set up laptops or tablets with safe access to the internet and invite the children to find out more about the persecuted church around the world. You may wish to decide which sites to use beforehand, to access only information which is age-appropriate.

Talk about the information the children discover and how we can use this to pray for Christians who are not allowed to worship openly. When we think about what happened to Daniel, we need to remember that God's followers are still punished today for choosing to follow him.

Creative

Inflate some balloons and provide newspaper, plain paper and a paste made with watered-down PVA glue. Invite the children to cover half of the balloon in papier mâché to create their own lion mask, leaving holes for the eyes and building up layers to form the nose. This project will require additional time, once the papier mâché has dried, for the children to paint their lion masks.

Talk about how Daniel must have felt when faced with the lions. He knew what the consequences of his actions would be, but still he chose to worship God.

Construction

Provide a small construction kit, such as Meccano, and challenge the children to build a den for the lions, perhaps providing some toy lions for the children to build a den around.

Talk about the way that King Darius used the lions as a punishment; but God is greater than any human threat and he saved Daniel from an expected death.

Writing

Provide writing paper and pens and invite the children to write a letter of encouragement. This could either be to a friend who is finding it difficult to follow God at the moment, encouraging them not to give up, or to an organisation working to support the persecuted church to thank them for the work they do, and to find out more about how we can pray for those in difficulties.

Talk about how we can encourage others to stand up for Jesus in a range of difficult circumstances, reminding them that they are not alone, but part of God's big family.

Books

Books provided today could include Bibles, children's story books about Daniel and the time spent in Babylon, as well as more contemporary testimonies of those who have faced difficulties or persecution as they live out their faith.

Talk about the things that interest the children when they look at the books, as appropriate, and be available to support those less able to read independently.

Prayer and reflective activity

Provide a number of dry-wipe pens in a selection of colours and invite the children to write or draw their prayers on the window glass. Dry-wipe pens work effectively on glass and can be wiped off easily.

Talk about Daniel who chose to pray at the window, even though he could be seen praying to God, which was why he was put in the lions' den. Daniel chose to worship God, even when it was hard.

Prayer

Father God, thank you for the example that Daniel set in choosing to honour you, even when he put his own life at risk. Help us to remember his bravery and courage when we find it challenging to live as your followers. Amen

Songs

Songs today could include:

- 'No other God' (Paul Jones)

Take home

Encourage the children to take some time, this week, to pray for all those Christians who live in parts of the world where it is difficult or challenging to live openly as a follower of God. You may wish to provide some additional information about those organisations which work to support persecuted Christians, if appropriate.

18

Jonah: God's messenger

For the team

Refer to pages 6–9 to see how the activity areas work together

Session theme

This session explores another of those stories often remembered from early childhood, but perhaps for the wrong reasons. This is not just a story about a boat and a big fish, but rather the story of God who gives second chances to all his people, because his love is greater than the things we do wrong.

Bible text: Jonah 1—4

Team prayer

Father God, thank you that no matter how many times we get things wrong, you always give us another chance to try again. Help us to listen to the things you say, and to share your message of love, hope and second chances with the people you send us out to meet. Amen

Story time

Since this is a longer story, you may find it works well to read it from a children's Bible or story book, or to retell the story in your own words. Ensure that the narrative you use includes all elements of the story, as the story ending is often missing in children's story books.

- What is your favourite part of the story and why?
- Can you relate to Jonah in any way?
- What would you have said to Jonah, if you had had the chance, at different points in the story?
- How can this story challenge us too?

Remind the children that we might want to criticise Jonah for the way he acted but, like us, he was only human, and sometimes found it hard to see things through God's eyes. God had to challenge Jonah in the way he was thinking. Sometimes he has to challenge us too.

Say: I wonder if there are times when we worry more about what other people are doing than what we are doing and how God feels about that. I wonder if we choose to do things sometimes because we think we know what God wants, even if we don't really know. Talk about the issues raised and how we can share God's message of love and hope with all people, listening carefully to the things that God asks us to do.

Drama

Divide the children into small groups and assign each group a segment of the story, perhaps as follows:

- God instructing Jonah to go to Nineveh
- Jonah escaping on a boat
- The storm at sea
- Jonah in the sea
- Jonah in the big fish
- Jonah arriving at Nineveh
- The crowd listening to Jonah and responding
- Jonah under the vine, listening to God

Ask each group to create a freeze frame for their part of the story, thinking particularly about Jonah, his thoughts and feelings at that moment.

Talk about the issues raised through this activity. Are there times when we feel like Jonah? What do you think we should do in these circumstances?

ICT

Set up laptops or tablets with safe access to the internet and invite the children to use map software to search for the places mentioned in the story.

Talk about how seeing where these places actually are helps bring the story to life. What do they know about these areas nowadays? How can we pray for them?

Creative

Provide squares of paper in an assortment of colours and work with the children to create origami whales and boats. You can find instructions on websites such as www.origami-instructions.com. The models could be put together on one large display or used by the children to help retell the story.

Talk about the significance of the big fish and the boat in the story. You could also discuss the way that origami starts to go wrong when we don't follow the instructions, just as things went wrong for Jonah when he didn't listen to God.

Construction

Provide a number of large cardboard boxes and extra wide sticky tape and challenge the children to work together as a group to build a large model boat, perhaps adding a mast and sail. They could complete the task as one large group or work as two competing teams.

Talk about the way that Jonah tried to get away from God by travelling in a boat in the opposite direction to the way that God told him to go. God is always with us and there is nowhere we can go to escape from him.

Books

Books offered today could include a selection of children's Bibles and story books which retell the story of Jonah, as well as some biblical and modern-day atlases in which the children can discover the locations of some of the places mentioned. Tarshish is believed to have been in southern Spain, and Nineveh in Iraq.

Talk about the things that interest the children when they look at the books, as appropriate, and be available to support those less able to read independently.

Prayer and reflective activity

Provide paper and pens and a large sand tray. Ask the children to write their name on the paper, before hiding it in the sand tray.

Talk about the way that just as Jonah tried to run away from God, we sometimes try to hide things about ourselves from him. God knew where Jonah was going and brought him safely back. How can we make sure that we do not hide from God but that we live our lives out in the open?

Games

Games played today could include the well-known game North, South, East, West, as a reminder of the time Jonah spent on a boat, and the way he tried to escape from God by travelling in the opposite direction to where he had been sent.

Prayer

Father God, thank you that no matter where we go or what we do, you love us and will always give us another chance. Help us to learn from the mistakes we make, to appreciate your love and forgiveness and to share this with other people. Amen

Songs

Songs today could include:

- 'I can do all things' (Jim Bailey)
- 'If I've been wrong' (Sammy Horner)

Take home

Challenge the children to ask God who they can speak to about him this week, and to have the courage to share a little of God's story with those people. Encourage the children to share how they get on with this at the next session.

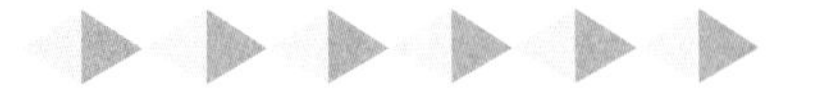

New Testament stories

19

Mary and the angel

For the team

Refer to pages 6–9 to see how the activity areas work together

Session theme

This is the first session exploring the stories of the New Testament, beginning with the promise of Jesus' birth. In this session, we consider Mary's response to the angel and how we, like Mary, can show obedience to God.

Bible text: Luke 1:26–38

Team prayer

Heavenly Father, thank you that you involve us in your plans, just as you involved Mary. Help us to trust you and to serve you willingly, just as Mary did. Amen

Story time

Share the story of the angel's appearance to Mary, from a children's story Bible or from an easy-to-read Bible translation.

- How do you think Mary felt when the angel appeared?
- What do you imagine Mary was thinking about when she heard this?
- How do you think you would respond, in Mary's position?
- How do you feel about this story?

Remind the children that Mary was a very young woman when this happened. She did not come from a well-known family or have any special training. When the angel appeared, it was a total surprise for Mary, but she listened carefully to what the angel said and willingly accepted the role she had to play.

Say: I wonder how you or I might react if an angel suddenly appeared in front of us! I wonder how we might react if the angel told us we had a special job to do for God. Mary accepted what the angel said and trusted that God would look after her when she did as he said. God will look after us when we trust him too.

Activity areas

Drama

Invite the children to play the following game with you. Each player stands in a space by themselves, relaxed and with their eyes closed. Explain that you will give the children an emotion, and on the signal, they should open their eyes and pose with the appropriate expression. For example, you may say 'excitement', before counting to three, when all the children should look excited. Use a range of different emotions for them to convey.

Talk about some of the different emotions, how the children best conveyed them and why we may feel them. What different emotions do you think Mary may have conveyed on this occasion?

ICT

Work together with the children to create a 'wobbly line' animation of the story. Create some simple drawings of Mary and the angel. Use a laptop, camera and motion grabbing software to capture images of the animation, ideally using a lightbox to set the position of the images, moving slightly each time to create the wobbly line technique. Since this animation technique takes a long time to capture, it would work well to create only a short scene, perhaps just the interaction between Mary and the angel.

Talk about how we can portray Mary's surprise and the sudden appearance of the angel in the animation that you create.

Creative

Provide thin card, pencils, pencil crayons and felt pens, for children to create their own Advent calendar (perhaps using the template on page 124), with key elements of the nativity story hidden behind each window.

Talk about how the story of Mary meeting the angel marks the start of the countdown to Christmas. Mary would need to wait several months, and had no idea how the story would evolve. We know what will happen, but there's still a lot to get excited about.

Construction

Together with the children, use chicken wire to construct a large angel-shaped frame, moulding and sculpting the appropriate shape. You could then use additional craft materials to cover the frame, such as different textured papers and fabrics.

Talk about the different times that angels are mentioned in the Bible, and how little we really know about their appearance. The images we have in our heads are based more on artwork or other people's ideas than on things that are actually said in the Bible.

Books

Provide a selection of nativity story books and children's Bibles, along with a selection of books about other biblical encounters with angels for the children to look at.

Talk about the things that interest the children when they look at the books, as appropriate, and be available to support those less able to read independently.

Prayer and reflective activity

Display the words of Mary's song (Luke 1:46–55) which some children may already be familiar with, depending upon your church tradition.

Talk about the way that these words flowed out of Mary when she went to visit her cousin, Elizabeth. What do these words mean to us today? How can we use them in our own prayers?

Games

Today, games which involve communicating messages would work well, such as Chinese Whispers, charades or Pictionary, as a reminder that the angel brought a message to Mary from God.

Prayer

Father God, thank you for Mary and for the way she played her part in your story. Help us to be willing to do the things you ask us to, just as Mary did. Amen

Songs

Songs today could include:

- 'Mary's song' (Richard Hubbard)

Take home

Invite the children to take their Advent calendars home and to use them as they count down to Christmas. Ask them to think about how they can remember Jesus' birth, and to prepare to celebrate the real meaning of Christmas.

20

Jesus is born

For the team

Refer to pages 6–9 to see how the activity areas work together

Session theme

This session celebrates one of the most central stories of our faith, and explores some of the myths around the nativity story, comparing them to the story contained in the Gospels. In this session, we celebrate the gift of Jesus, and how God came to dwell among his people.

Bible text: Luke 2:1–20

Team prayer

Father God, thank you for the gift of your Son, Jesus, who became a man and dwelt among us. May we remember and celebrate the reason for the Christmas season, and share this joy with all those we meet. Amen

Story time

Read the story with the children, from an age-appropriate children's Bible story book or an easy-to-read translation. Encourage the children to look closely at the story as it is told in the Bible, rather than relying on what they think they know from hearing the story at Christmas each year.

- What was your favourite part of the story?
- What surprises you most?
- What would you like to know, that you don't read about in this passage?
- Why do you think Jesus' birth happened in this way?

Discuss the children's ideas and questions raised from the story.

Say: I wonder how this story makes you feel. I wonder how the shepherds felt that night, or how Mary and Joseph felt. This is a story we enjoy hearing every year, perhaps because it reminds us of good memories or helps us to celebrate Christmas in some way. This story is central to this time of year; it's the very reason why we celebrate in the first place. I wonder how we can remember Jesus at the centre of our celebrations.

Drama

Recap the details of the nativity story from the Bible passage, before setting the children the challenge of creating their own nativity play but retold in a modern context. Challenge them to think of a contemporary equivalent of a stable, the shepherds, the wise men, and so on.

Talk about how different the story would be if Jesus was born today. How does retelling the story in a different context help us to better understand the meaning of events? Does anything lose its meaning?

ICT

Provide a drawing programme for the children to create and print their own Christmas cards, depicting elements of the nativity story or key Bible verses relating to the Christmas story. This could be a guided or free activity, as you wish. Perhaps you could provide some published Christmas cards in a variety of styles, as a stimulus for the children's own designs.

Talk about the way that many published Christmas cards use medieval art to show the nativity scene. There are many other ways that we can show the story, and our own designs can help to tell it in a fresh way.

Creative

Provide a selection of peg dolls, as well as very small paintbrushes and paints (acrylic paints are particularly effective but watercolour paints can also be used). Invite the children to paint their own nativity scene figures, either individually or working with others to create a set which can be put together.

Talk about the different characters and the roles each of them played in the story, as the children choose which character to represent.

Construction

Gather pieces of scrap wood, perhaps pieces of recycled pallets, or cut-offs of wood that you can source as well as nails and other woodworking tools. Work together with the children to build a manger, using photographs or pictures of a manger as a stimulus for the construction.

Talk about the care that parents take choosing a cot or crib for their newborn babies. Joseph, the carpenter, may well have made a crib for Jesus at home, but now Jesus had to spend his first night sleeping in an animal's feeding trough!

Writing

Provide small strips of coloured paper to use to make paper chains, along with pens and a stapler. Invite the children to write a name that describes who Jesus is to them, on one of the strips of paper. Then loop the strips together, fastening them with the stapler. Once complete, the paper chains could be hung around the room.

Talk about the different names for Jesus that the children know, such as 'Messiah' or 'Christ', and discuss what each of these names means.

Books

Display a selection of different story books retelling the events of the first Christmas, perhaps including some which have been written for younger children, together with some Bibles, and encourage the children to look closely to see which tales accurately retell the story of Jesus' birth.

Share the books with the children and discuss the things they discover. Why do some retellings include additional or changed details? Is it all right to retell part of the story differently?

Prayer and reflective activity

Gather a number of small boxes, along with Christmas wrapping paper, gift labels, pens, scissors and sticky tape. Invite the children to come and wrap up a gift to give to Jesus, thinking about what they would put into their box if they could give Jesus any gift at all. They may wish to write down what they would give to Jesus, before putting this into the box that they wrap. The children can then write a label, with a message to Jesus.

Talk about the children's own ideas about what would make a good gift for Jesus, thinking about him either as a baby or as the man he became. What could we give to the God who created everything?

Games

Prepare a nativity story quiz to help the children explore which of the details in the story are in the original text and which are not. This could be done as a series of 'True or false?' statements, such as 'There was a donkey in the story' (False) and 'Jesus was laid in a manger' (True).

Prayer

Father God, thank you for Christmas and for the gift of your Son, Jesus. In the middle of our parties and special events, help us to remember the reason why we celebrate at this time of year. Amen

Songs

Songs today could include:

- 'Come and join the celebration' (Valerie Collinson)
- 'Oh what a day' (Nick and Becky Drake)

Take home

Encourage the children to take home their peg doll nativity scene characters and to create a space in their own home where a nativity scene can be set up for the whole family to see, as a reminder of the reason for our Christmas celebrations.

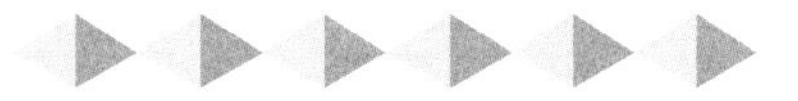

21 Jesus in the temple

For the team

Refer to pages 6–9 to see how the activity areas work together

Session theme

This session and the Bible passage provide a brief glimpse into Jesus' childhood, where we discover the boy who was growing in understanding in a way that surprised the adults around him. Through this session, we discover how, as children, we can follow the example that he set in his thirst to learn and to grow.

Bible text: Luke 2:41–52

Team prayer

Dear Jesus, thank you that you became human, providing the perfect role model for us all. Help us to thirst and to long for you, and to grow to become more like you. Amen

Story time

Share the story with the children, perhaps while preparing the drama activity, as detailed below, from an appropriate Bible translation, or children's story Bible.

- How does this story make you feel?
- How do you think the different characters would have felt as these events took place?
- What do we discover about Jesus from this story?
- What does this story teach us about following Jesus' example?

Explain to the children that this is the only story we have about Jesus as a child, but it tells us so much about him and the things that mattered to him. Sometimes we forget that Jesus was fully human, as well as fully God. That can be a really difficult idea to get our heads around, but this story can help. It shows us how Jesus was a child, like us, whose parents were worried when he went missing, and how he stood out when he surprised the teachers in the temple, because of the things that he already knew and understood about God.

Say: I wonder who learned most about God that day—Jesus, his parents or the rabbis. I wonder what we can learn from this story about what it means to be a follower of God. As we grow up physically, we also grow spiritually, becoming more and more like Jesus.

Drama

Provide copies of the story, either directly from the Bible or from a children's story Bible, and challenge the children to work together to create a news report of the story. The children could play the roles of newsreaders, reporters, Mary, Joseph, rabbis in the temple, Jesus and other eyewitnesses, as appropriate. You could help the children to write a script ready to perform or to ad lib, as appropriate. You could also provide a selection of props and costumes.

Talk about the different issues raised from the story as you prepare your drama sketch, thinking about the different emotions felt by the key characters at each point in the story, and what we discover about Jesus from this particular episode.

ICT

Provide a simple video camera which the children can use to film and record the news report created in the drama activity above. You could divide the children into separate groups; one to create the drama and another to film and edit a recording of the news report. The children involved in the ICT activity could direct the filming, thinking about the locations that you use, and any sound effects or special effects that they could use to enhance the recording.

As the children prepare the recording of the story, talk about the details that are important to focus on. Who could they share this recording with? How do they want to share the story with their audience?

Construction

Provide a supply of small building bricks, together with base boards and a few marbles. Invite the children to construct their own marble maze, using the building bricks, on one of the base boards. The children can then share their marble mazes with one another, for them to test out.

Talk about the children's own experiences of being lost, like the marble caught in the maze. Mary and Joseph were very worried about what had happened to Jesus, but he didn't think he was lost and was surprised by their reaction.

Writing

Cut out some large question mark shapes from coloured paper and provide pens. Invite the children to write their own questions for God, or questions about God, which can then be displayed on the walls for everyone to see, explaining that Jesus asked the leaders in the temple lots of questions to help him to learn more about God.

Talk about the different questions the children have and where they may be able to find the answers to some of these.

Books

Display a selection of books for the children to explore. For this session, books could include a selection of Bibles and Bible story books, as well as books that help us to discover more about the Bible, such as appropriate encyclopaedias and atlases.

Share the books with the children, discussing the things that they find interesting. Talk about the way that Jesus wanted to learn more about the scriptures, and how we can discover more by looking at books like these.

Prayer and reflective activity

Ask one of the leaders to bring in some personal photographs, from the time when they were a young child through to the present day.

As the children look at the photos, talk about how the leader has grown and changed through the years and about the different people who helped them to grow and develop, particularly spiritually. Who helped Jesus to grow? Who helps us to grow? Thank God for those people.

Games

Games that involve asking questions would work well in this session, such as the yes/no game, where a leader asks a player a list of questions, which they can answer with anything except the words 'yes' or 'no'. You could also set up the board game Guess Who? for children to play, asking more questions.

Prayer

Dear Jesus, thank you that you experienced life as a human being, living through many of the same things that we do—having friends, learning things from other people and being in a family. Help us, as we grow, to become more like you. Amen

Songs

Songs today could include:

- 'I love my Dad' (Dave Godfrey)

Take home

Suggest that the children take some of their big God questions, from the writing activity, away with them today. Encourage them to think about who they could share their questions with, and to share what they have found out when they come to the next session.

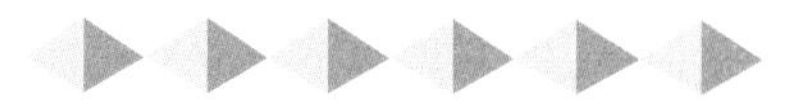

22 Jesus' baptism

For the team

Refer to pages 6–9 to see how the activity areas work together

Session theme

In this session, we see the Trinity of God, Father, Son and Holy Spirit together in one place and we see Jesus, about to embark on his great ministry in the world, recognised by his own cousin as the promised Messiah. In this session, we explore some of our own baptism traditions, and how these follow in Jesus' footsteps.

Bible text: Matthew 3:13–17

Team prayer

Lord Jesus, thank you for the way that you willingly walked the path set out for you. May we be prepared to walk in your footsteps as children of God, ready to do the things that you ask of us. Amen

Story time

Share today's story with the children, either reading from a Bible or a children's Bible story book.

- What is most surprising about this story?
- What do we learn about God?
- Why do you think John responded in the way he did?
- What does this story teach us about baptism?

Explain to the children that Jesus' baptism marked a beginning for him—the start of his ministry on earth. Through this story, we also see the Trinity of God in one place. This can be a really difficult idea for us to understand, as we often separate God into Father, Son and Spirit as seen in different stories, but there is one God. Discuss this idea further with the children, as appropriate.

Say: I wonder what it meant for Jesus to hear Father God say, 'I am pleased with you.' I wonder what it would mean for us to hear that Father God is pleased with us. God has accepted us as his children, as members of his family. We can follow in Jesus' footsteps and do great things for God with his Holy Spirit working in us.

Drama

Set up a chair which can be used as a hot seat and ask a volunteer to play the part of John, and to sit in the chair. Model how you can act as an interviewer to ask John questions about what happened on the day that Jesus was baptised, before inviting the other children to act as the interviewer and ask John further questions. You could repeat the exercise with a different child playing the part of John, as time allows.

Talk about John's experiences that day, and how he may respond to some of the questions the children ask, as you complete this activity together.

ICT

Work together with the children to create a short video or a PowerPoint presentation to explain baptism. Tell the children they are creating a resource which could be used to explain baptism to their friends. They could include an explanation of how baptism is celebrated in your own church tradition as well as other baptism traditions, as appropriate.

Talk about what details the children wish to include in the presentation, and the issues, ideas and questions that this raises, encouraging them to share their own experiences of baptism and any questions they may have.

Creative

Provide squares of white paper and work with the children to create origami doves together. You can find instructions to follow on websites such as www.origami-instructions.com. Allow for mistakes and trial and error, and provide extra paper for the children to work with until they are happy with the doves that they make.

Talk about the dove that appeared in the sky when Jesus was baptised, as a sign of the Holy Spirit descending.

Construction

Provide a selection of different junk modelling objects made from a variety of different materials and challenge the children to work in small groups to construct a model of the river, which can hold water without leaking.

Talk about the way John baptised people in the river. Nowadays, people are usually baptised inside a building, but some are still baptised in a river or in the sea.

Books

Books offered for the children to read today could include books about different baptism traditions, alongside children's Bibles and story books about Jesus' time on earth.

Share the books with the children, supporting the children as needed, and talking about the issues and questions that are raised.

Prayer and reflective activity

Display a selection of artefacts relating to baptism and how you celebrate it in your church tradition. These may include a candle, shell, oil, and so on. If possible, show the children the font or baptistry pool which you use for baptisms at your church.

Talk about each of the artefacts; what they mean and how they are used. Encourage the children to share their own stories and questions about baptism and talk about the way that we are following in Jesus' footsteps when we are baptised.

Games

Set up a small pool of water and into it drop a number of objects which relate to the story. These could include a plastic dove, a sandal, a plastic locust (for John!), a play figure or laminated picture of John and Jesus, and so on. Divide the children into two small teams and give each team a fishing net. On the signal to go, each team should begin a relay race, to fish the objects out of the water.

Talk about the different objects, how they relate to the story, and how different Jesus' baptism was from our own experiences of baptism.

Prayer

Dear Jesus, thank you for the example that you set, always doing the things that Father God asked of you. Help us, as we follow in your footsteps, to do the things that you need us to do. Amen

Songs

Songs today could include:

- 'You are my son' (Dave Godfrey)

Take home

Suggest that the children could ask their friends and family members to share their own baptism stories with them, perhaps looking at family photos or videos, and talking about what baptism means to them.

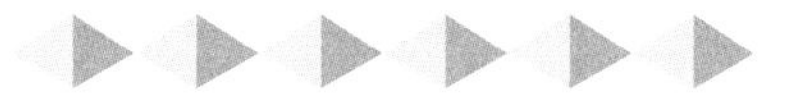

23

Jesus chooses his disciples

For the team

Refer to pages 6–9 to see how the activity areas work together

Session theme

During this session we discover how Jesus invited some of his first disciples to follow him as he began his ministry, and we are reminded that the same invitation to follow Jesus stands for us today.

Bible text: Luke 5:1–11

Team prayer

Lord Jesus, thank you that you invite us to follow you, learning on the job, just as those first disciples did. Help us to extend this invitation to those we meet and work with, on our own discipleship journey. Amen

Story time

Look at the Bible passage together, from an appropriate Bible translation or children's Bible story book.

- How do you think Simon and the others felt when Jesus first spoke to them about fishing?
- Why do you think they so willingly followed Jesus?
- How do you think you would have responded in that situation?
- What does this story teach us about being a disciple?

Explain to the children that Jesus would invite twelve men to join him as his disciples, followers or learners. They would work with Jesus for the next three years, learning about what it meant to be a follower of God and discovering how Jesus would change the world by his life and time on earth.

Say: I wonder how the fishermen first felt when they left their nets to follow Jesus. I wonder who other people would have expected Jesus to choose as his followers. The same invitation that was given to Jesus' first disciples is there for us too. We can become followers of Jesus, learning more about the things that he said and did and putting them into action in our own lives.

Drama

After exploring the story together, work with the children to create a sketch exploring what would have happened if Jesus had held job interviews before appointing the disciples to the role, rather than simply inviting them to follow him. You could perhaps think about the different types of people you could interview for the role, as well as the different questions you might expect Jesus to ask.

Talk about how surprising it is that Jesus actually did nothing like this, choosing instead to invite a group of ordinary men to become his followers and join him in his work. Why do you think he did things this way?

ICT

Set up a laptop or tablet with secure access to the internet and find an appropriate online 'learning styles' questionnaire for the children to use. Once the questionnaire is completed, children may wish to print out their results to discuss further.

Talk about the fact that different people learn best in different ways. Jesus invites us to learn from him when we become his followers. Once we know the ways in which we learn best, how can we use that knowledge to help us learn more about being a follower of God?

Creative

Source some long, thin modelling balloons and a balloon pump and show the children how to inflate a balloon to create a simple balloon fish. You can find instructions on websites such as www.balloonotherapy.blogspot.com. Gather the fish together as the children make them, perhaps storing them in large nets (see the Construction activity below).

Talk about the way that Jesus stopped the fishermen in their tracks and offered them a whole new lifestyle. Would we give up the things that we know so easily?

Construction

Using some long lengths of rope, work with the children to create a net, knotting the ropes at the appropriate intersections. If you have leaders with the appropriate skills, you could teach the children a variety of different knots which they could try out with the rope.

Talk about the way that the disciples would have spent hours repairing and caring for their nets because they were so necessary to their jobs. Leaving them behind would have been a big change for them.

Books

Provide a selection of children's Bibles and books which retell some of the stories of Jesus and his disciples. You could also provide a selection of autobiographies of well-known Christians from more recent history for the children to look at.

Share the books with the children, helping them with reading as necessary, and talking about how these stories can inspire and encourage us, as followers of Jesus.

Prayer and reflective activity

Provide some white squares of card, together with a hole-punch, string and red felt pens and invite the children to make a set of L-plates for themselves to wear. As they do so, explain that one of the meanings of the word 'disciple' is to be a learner—somebody who is learning from a teacher.

Talk about what it means for us to be disciples or learners, with Jesus as our teacher. What lessons have you or the children learned recently, which you can share with one another?

Games

Group games played today could include the well-known Cod, Herring, Mackerel, Plaice, where children sit on chairs in a circle, facing outwards, and are assigned one of the four fish names. When their fish name is called, all the children in that group run around the circle in the same direction. Then, when the leader calls 'Tide's turning', the children change direction and run the other way. When the leader calls 'Fisherman's coming', the children try to return to their original position. If you wish, the last player to return to their chair each time can be called 'out', turning their chair to face the centre of the circle.

Prayer

Dear Jesus, thank you that you invite us to become your followers, always learning more from you, just as those first disciples did. Help us to stay close to you, following in your footsteps and learning from the lessons that you teach us. Amen

Songs

Songs today could include:

- 'Jesus, Superhero' (Nigel Hemming)

Take home

Challenge the children, in the week that follows, to ask one other Christian who they know what it means to them to be a disciple or a follower of Jesus. You could make space, during the next session, for the children to share what they have discovered.

24 The wise and foolish builders

For the team

Refer to pages 6–9 to see how the activity areas work together

Session theme

This session explores one of the most well-known of Jesus' parables—the wise and foolish builders—and helps the children to discover what it means to build our lives on good foundations.

Bible text: Matthew 7:24–29

Team prayer

Lord Jesus, thank you for the things that you teach us. Help us to build our lives upon your teaching as a firm foundation, steady and secure even when things get tough. Amen

Story time

Share the story together, perhaps from a children's Bible or Bible story book. If you prefer, you could combine this discussion time with the drama activity, as described below.

- Why do you think Jesus told this story?
- What sorts of things are like the sandy foundations?
- What does it mean to build your house on the rock?
- How does this story challenge us today?

Remind the children that when Jesus was teaching people he often told stories, or parables, that people would have to think about to help them to learn something important. Jesus was a fantastic storyteller: he could keep the crowds listening for a long time, and challenged them through the messages of the stories.

Say: I wonder whether you think you are building your life on rock or sand. I wonder how you feel when the storms come, as they did in the story. Jesus promises us that if we build our lives on him, trusting in the things that he said, we will be safe and secure no matter what difficulties we go through, just like the man who built his house on the rock.

Drama

Ask for two volunteers to play the parts of the wise and foolish builders and provide a number of building blocks that can be used as props. Explain to the rest of the group that they should provide sound effects at the appropriate points in the story, such as the weather and the house crashing down. Read the story from the Bible, and ask the two volunteers to perform an impromptu narrated drama, responding to the story as you read it.

Talk about the things that the children noticed from the story. This story is straightforward to understand. How does it challenge us to think about the way that we live?

ICT

Set up a laptop or tablet with a drawing or design package (free software can be downloaded) and invite the children to use this to design their own 'dream home'.

Talk about the children's ideas for what would make their dream home and what they would include in the design. If you cared that much about the home you had designed, you would take extra care over how and where it was built, to ensure that it would stand the test of time.

Creative

Provide a selection of collaging materials, including different papers, fabrics, paints, scissors and glue, and work together as a group to create a picture that portrays this parable. As you do so, think about what the different elements of the story represent—particularly the rocky ground, the sandy ground and the stormy weather—and how you can portray them in the picture.

Talk about how representing this story visually can help us to understand better what Jesus was saying through it.

Construction

Provide a selection of small building bricks and base boards and invite the children to design and build their own model of their dream house. Encourage the children to use as detailed and intricate a design as they are able, and set the completed models out on display.

Talk about the children's different ideas and designs. If you were building something that mattered this much to you, what would you do to ensure that you achieved the desired effect?

Books

Display a selection of children's Bibles and age-appropriate retellings of this and other parables. You could also provide a selection of non-fiction books about architecture, perhaps including design books with photographs of different buildings.

Share the books with the children, talking about the way that Jesus taught people through the stories that he told, and how stories can help us to think about the things that Jesus said. As you look at the architecture books, talk about the time that engineers spend getting their building projects right. How much more important is it for us to build our lives on good foundations?

Prayer and reflective activity

Provide a basic outline drawing of the house built on rock and the house built on sand. Invite the children to write, in the house built on sand, their own ideas about the unstable or unreliable things that we sometimes build our lives on. You could also invite them to write their names inside the house built on the rock as a sign of their commitment to trusting Jesus.

Talk about the children's own ideas about the types of things that can give way and cannot be trusted as a foundation for our lives, as well as what it means to build our lives trusting in Jesus as a good foundation.

Games

Games provided for the children today could include Jenga or Giant Jenga, along with other balancing or tumbling games.

Prayer

Dear Jesus, thank you for the stories that you told which teach us as much today as they taught the first disciples. Help us to build our lives on solid rock, trusting in you above all else. Amen

Songs

Songs today could include:

- 'I'm gonna build my life on solid rock' (Andrew and Pauline Pearson)

Take home

Challenge the children, when they get home, to think about the different things that they depend upon as their 'foundations', and to consider whether they need to change any of these things. How are they trusting in God? Where are they depending on more sandy soil?

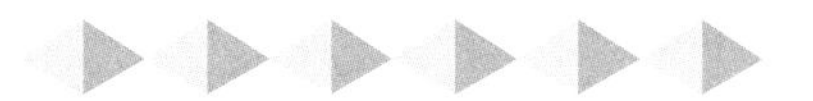

25

Jesus heals a paralysed man

For the team

Refer to pages 6–9 to see how the activity areas work together

Session theme

This session tells the story of one of Jesus' healing miracles. Through this session, we consider how God has power to heal, as well as thinking about what it means to bring our friends to Jesus, just as the friends of the man in the story did, and how Jesus can change their lives.

Bible text: Mark 2:1–17

Team prayer

Lord Jesus, thank you for those people who took time to introduce us to you. Thank you for the privilege of bringing these children to meet you for themselves. Today, may we help them to understand the role that they play in bringing their friends to you. Amen

Story time

Share the story together, looking at the text in the Bible or reading the story from a Bible story book.

- What surprises you most about this story?
- How do you think the paralysed man and his friends would have felt at each stage of the story?
- What did the crowds discover about Jesus?
- What unanswered questions does this story leave you with?

Remind the children that there are lots of stories in the Bible of Jesus healing people, and we know that he still heals people today. But we also know that sometimes people are not healed when we pray for them and sometimes this can be hard to understand. You may wish to discuss this in more detail with the children, as appropriate.

Say: I wonder how we can follow the example of the men in this story and introduce our friends to Jesus. I wonder what we might ask Jesus to do for them. Jesus wants to meet with people today, just as he did when he walked on earth. We can introduce our friends to him by telling them what it means to be a follower of Jesus and talking about how Jesus helps us with our own lives.

Drama

After exploring the story together, ask the children to set up an interview situation with key characters from the story. Together, they should generate a selection of questions to ask. Then, one child could play the role of a journalist, asking questions of children playing the witnesses to the scene, to find out more of what happened on that day.

Talk about the way that different characters would have had different perspectives on what happened that day, from the man and his friends to the onlookers in the crowd. Not everyone would have been happy with what Jesus said and did. How can you explain and explore these perspectives?

ICT

Set up a computer or laptop, perhaps with access to a printer, and invite the children to work together to create a newspaper article. This could include material created through the interviews the children generated in the drama activity to form eyewitness statements, as well as taking details from the Bible story.

Talk about the way that this story would still have made the news today and why the children think that may be. Why do you think we sometimes keep quiet about the different things that God does in our lives? How can we be more ready to share our stories?

Creative

Provide some simple templates that the children can use to create a jointed person, using split pins at each of the joints to enable the person to move (see page 125). These figures can be purchased in kit form if you prefer. You will also need pens or pencils for the children to use to colour their people.

Talk about the way that Jesus healed the man, enabling him to move, just as the jointed man can now move.

Construction

Invite the children to construct a model of the flat-roofed house, perhaps from building bricks, cardboard boxes or wooden pallets. Remind them to include a staircase up to the roof and invite them to dig a hole in the roof, as the friends would have done to lower the paralysed man through.

Talk about how this style of house, with its flat roof, is different from the ones we are used to. The story tells us that so many people had come to see Jesus that the only way they could get near to him was to go through the roof.

Writing

Provide a selection of 'Get well soon' or 'Thinking of you' cards or craft materials for the children to make their own. Invite the children to write a card to send to a friend or family member, as appropriate.

Talk about the way that God cares about our friends who are unwell or finding things difficult, just as he cared for the man who was brought to see him. You may wish to discuss further the issues raised by the children and this story at this point.

Books

Display a selection of Bibles and children's story Bibles, together with other story books which tell some of the stories of how Jesus healed people. You may also be able to provide a selection of more contemporary testimonies of people who have experienced physical healing through prayer.

Share the books with the children, supporting them with reading as needed, and discussing the issues raised by these books, particularly themes of healing and the questions this raises.

Prayer and reflective activity

Provide pieces of paper and pens and invite the children to write the names of their friends on the paper; people who they want to bring close to Jesus, just as the friends in the story brought the man to Jesus.

Talk about what we can do to bring our friends closer to Jesus and why we want to do this. Pray with the children for opportunities to share our stories with our friends and to tell them more about him.

Prayer

Lord Jesus, thank you for the people who bring us to meet you, for our friends and our family. Help us to find opportunities to bring our friends to meet you too, whether it is through groups like this one, sharing stories with them or talking about the things that you have done for us. Amen

Songs

Songs today could include:

- 'I want to be like Jesus' (Cindy Rethmeier)

Take home

Challenge the children to pray for an opportunity, in the week ahead, to do one thing to bring their friends closer to Jesus, perhaps inviting them to come along to this group or to another special event, or to share a story of something that Jesus has done for them.

26

The farmer and his seeds

For the team

Refer to pages 6–9 to see how the activity areas work together

Session theme

This session explores one of Jesus' parables, that of the sower who went to sow some seeds. There are two ways to view this story—that we ourselves are the types of soil or that we are the sower who has a basket full of seeds to sow. This session explores both these themes, challenging the children to think about how they can take responsibility for growing their own faith and how they can sow seeds into other people's lives too.

Bible text: Mark 4:1–9, 13–20

Team prayer

Lord Jesus, our teacher, thank you for the stories you told and the lessons we can learn from them. Help us to retell these stories in a way that the children can understand and be challenged by, as we are. Amen

Story time

Use an appropriate Bible translation or a children's Bible story book to share the story together.

- What makes this story easy or more difficult for us to understand?
- How can you relate to the story?
- Can you imagine some of your friends as the different sorts of soil?
- How does this parable challenge you?

Remind the children that Jesus often chose to tell stories or parables to teach the crowds of people who followed him. He knew that everyone who heard his stories would be really listening to what he had to say. This parable reminds us that everyone can hear God's message, but that it is up to us what we choose to do with it.

Say: I wonder what type of soil we are. I wonder what happens when we sow seeds into our friends' lives. Jesus taught that everyone should have the opportunity to hear his message, but that it is up to us what happens next. Are we growing well? What should we do about that?

Drama

Divide the children into four smaller groups and explain that each group will need to mime what happened to the seeds which were sown in the different areas. Share the story with the children, helping them to see what happened to the seeds that were planted in each of the different places, and how they can physically mime this. Once they have had time to rehearse their actions, read the parable together as a group, inviting each group to share their mime at the appropriate point.

Talk about the different soil types mentioned in the parable and how each of these represents what happens when different people hear God's message and how they respond to God's story. Discuss any issues that this parable raises for the children.

ICT

Provide a digital camera and go out into the local area with the children. Ask them to look for each of the different soil types mentioned in the parable, and to photograph the best examples they find. Alternatively, you could provide safe access to the internet for the children to search for appropriate images online if an outdoor visit is not feasible.

Talk about what the children notice when they find each of the different soil types. How does seeing these things for ourselves help us to better understand what Jesus was saying?

Creative

Gather some plain plant pots and provide acrylic paints for the children to use to decorate the pots, before filling with compost and sowing seeds in them. Choose an easy-to-grow seed, appropriate to the season, which children can take care of at home, perhaps returning them to the group once they are fully grown.

Talk about what the children will need to do in order to care for their growing seeds at home. How can we care for the seeds that have been sown in our own lives as we learn more about what it means to follow God?

Construction

Provide a number of different straws, both plastic and paper, and masking tape and challenge the children to join the straws end to end, taping them together to create the longest working straw that they can. Provide some glasses of water for the children to use to test their straws, as they complete the challenge.

Talk about the way that plants set down roots into the soil and use them to take in the water and nutrients that they need to grow. How can we set down good roots? What sorts of things will help us to grow in our faith?

Writing

Provide some examples of different seed packets, along with templates for the children to use to make their own seed packet from paper (see page 126). Invite the children to write their own set of instructions on their packet to explain how we should best care for the seeds that have been sown in our own lives.

Talk about some of the things we can do to nurture our faith, protecting it from the things which may try to stop us from growing, and encouraging it to grow by putting the right support in place.

Books

Display a selection of books including Bibles and children's story Bibles, as well as story books telling this and other parables of Jesus.

Talk about the things that interest the children when they look at the books, as appropriate, and be available to support those less able to read independently. Talk about the way Jesus taught the people through the stories that he told, and how we can still learn from these stories today.

Prayer and reflective activity

Provide a large sack or bag of seed and smaller bags for the children to scoop seeds into, ready to take away with them.

Talk about the opportunities that the children have to sow seeds into other people's lives, and tell them a little about Jesus. This could be their friends or family members. Remind the children of the farmer in the story who sowed his seed widely, and how we can do the same.

Games

Divide the children into two teams and provide each team with a basket, perhaps a laundry basket, with a number of small balls inside it (a different colour for each team). Each team should try to empty their basket of balls, while at the same time scooping the opposing team's balls back into their basket. The winning team is the first to empty their basket of balls, just as the farmer emptied his bag of seeds.

Prayer

Dear Jesus, thank you that people have taken time to sow seeds into our own lives, so that we may discover more about you. Help us to take the opportunities you give each of us to sow seeds into other people's lives too. Amen

Songs

Songs today could include:

- 'Sow 'n' sow' (Ian Smale)

Take home

Remind the children to take home their planted seeds from the creative activity, and their bag of seed from the prayer and reflective activity. As they care for their growing seedling, encourage them to think both about what they are doing to grow healthily as a follower of Jesus, and about how they are giving other people the opportunity to hear more about Jesus.

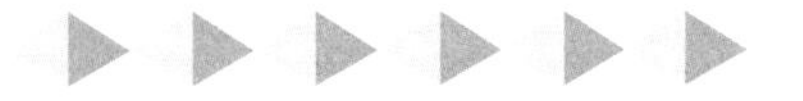

27

Jesus feeds 5000 people

For the team

Refer to pages 6–9 to see how the activity areas work together

Session theme

In this session we discover what happened when Jesus fed a crowd with one small boy's lunch. Through the activities, we consider how we all have something to offer to God, and how he can do unimaginable things with our small offerings.

Bible text: Mark 6:30–44

Team prayer

Dear Jesus, thank you that you take the small gifts that we have, and can multiply them beyond our wildest imaginings. May we bring what little we have to you, just as the boy in the story did, so that you can use it to do great things. Amen

Story time

Provide age-appropriate Bibles or an age-appropriate Bible story book for the children to look at this story together. This discussion could also be based around the drama activity, as described below.

- Why do you think the crowds were so keen to stay with Jesus?
- How do you think the boy would have felt when he had the opportunity to share his food?
- Who do you think was most surprised by what happened?
- What does this story teach us about Jesus?

Explain to the children that Jesus performed many miracles while he was on earth, of which this was just one, when Jesus shocked the crowds by performing the impossible.

Say: I wonder what we would have done if we were in the crowd that day. I wonder what we can offer to Jesus to play our part in his story. In this story, we discover how Jesus took the small offering that one boy had to share and used it to feed the whole crowd, involving that boy in his plans. This shows us that we can all have a part to play in God's story, with whatever small things we have to bring.

Drama

Work with the children to generate a list of key words that they find in the Bible story and to create an action or sound that they can put together with each of the words. As you read the passage to the children, encourage them to perform their action or sound effect each time you read the given word.

Talk about the things that the children notice from the story as you read it together, and any questions or issues raised.

ICT

Provide laptops or tablets with access to a range of clipart images. Challenge the children to create a picture which shows a crowd of 5000 people. They may find an image of a small crowd which they can count, before duplicating as needed to create an image of 5000 people.

Talk about what 5000 actually looks like when they see how many people they have included in the image. The crowd was so great because so many people wanted to hear Jesus speak and didn't want to go home to eat.

Creative

Working with the children, follow a simple recipe to make a loaf of bread together (perhaps using a quick bread recipe). If you have no baking facilities, you could just provide a dough mixture, playdough or salt dough, so that children can explore the texture.

Talk about the process of making bread and the effort that goes into the job. Who do you think made the bread for the boy in the story? They could not have imagined what Jesus would do with it, to feed the crowds.

Construction

Gather some resources that can be used for basket weaving, such as willow, perhaps from a basket weaving kit, and invite the children to help you to weave a basket together. (Larger groups could perhaps be set the challenge of trying to weave all twelve baskets, as used in the story.)

Talk about the way that the disciples were able to collect twelve full baskets of leftovers after everybody had eaten. This was no mean picnic; there was plenty of food for everyone!

Books

Display a selection of children's Bibles and Bible story books, along with story books which retell some of the other miracles performed by Jesus.

Talk about the things that interest the children when they look at the books, as appropriate, and be available to support those less able to read independently.

Prayer and reflective activity

Set out the baskets created by the children in the construction activity and provide paper and pens. Invite the children to write something which they can offer to God on a piece of paper, before putting it into the basket.

Talk about the different things that the children feel they can bring to God, helping them to explore some of these ideas, and what opportunities God gives us to use these different gifts.

Challenge

Set up a fun times-table quiz, not putting children under pressure to answer, but giving those children for whom this is a strength an opportunity to join in, perhaps using a first-to-the-buzzer approach. Remind the children that Jesus multiplied the boy's gifts to feed the crowd.

Prayer

Dear Jesus, thank you that you can take the little gifts that we offer and multiply them into something fantastic, just as you did with the boy's tiny lunch box. Amen

Songs

Songs today could include:

- 'Only a boy' (Richard Hubbard)
- 'Your eyes' (David Wakerly, Beci Wakerly and Julia A'Bell)

Take home

Provide a small fish-shaped piece of paper for the children to take home with them, as a reminder of this session, and the way that Jesus took what the boy had and multiplied it for everyone. They could write the things they can offer to Jesus on this fish shape, as they have done on the piece of paper they put into the basket during the session.

28 The good Samaritan

Refer to pages 6–9 to see how the activity areas work together

For the team

Session theme

This session explores one of Jesus' better-known parables and challenges us to think about those people we may normally choose to ignore. Through the activities we explore how we can be a good neighbour to all, regardless of status or background, showing love to everyone.

Bible text: Luke 10:25–37

Team prayer

Lord Jesus, for the times when we do not live out the things that you teach us, we are sorry. May we share honestly the times when we find your teachings challenging, and encourage the children with whom we work to do the same. Amen

Story time

Share the story with the children from an appropriate Bible translation or Bible story book, or encourage the children to discuss the points raised as they complete the drama activity below.

- Why do you think the man asked this question?
- How do you think the people who heard the story would have reacted to what Jesus was saying?
- Why do you think Jesus chose to tell this story?
- How does this story challenge us?

Explain to the children that this story would have been very powerful to those who first heard it. Jesus chose to tell the story, using groups of people that the audience would have been familiar with, to help them understand what it meant to really love our neighbour. You may wish to explain this in more detail and explain who Jesus was referring to in the story.

Say: I wonder who we could put into the story to make it as challenging for us today. I wonder who we might be challenged to show love for, as a neighbour. Jesus was not just telling a feel-good story; he was challenging his listeners to understand that being a neighbour, as God wanted, meant showing extravagant love to the most unlikely people.

Drama

Explore the parable together from the Bible text before setting the children the challenge of retelling it in a modern context. Encourage the children to think about who would take the place of the key characters if Jesus were telling the story today.

Talk about how this parable is still as powerful and challenging now as it was at the time when Jesus first told it. How does changing some of the details to bring it up to date help us to better understand the meaning of the parable?

ICT

If possible, take the children out into the local area (this activity can be combined with the prayer and reflective activity) to take some digital photos to show what makes up your neighbourhood.

Talk about who your neighbours really are. How well do you know the different groups represented in your local area? What can you do to get to know them better?

Creative

Use the photographs taken in the ICT activity, together with a selection of pictures taken from magazines and newspapers, to create a collage of 'our neighbours', both on a local and a global scale.

Talk about how we are connected to all these people. What is it that brings us all together? How can we show neighbourly love to these people, even when they are far away from us?

Construction

Source a large number of small building bricks and ask the children to construct a detailed model of the scene, showing the road from Jerusalem to Jericho and what occurred there in this parable. Provide Bibles or copies of the story for the children to use as they decide what to include in their model.

Talk about what happened in the story and the significance of the location of the events. Why did Jesus choose to include a Samaritan as the hero of the tale? What does this story tell us about how we judge others?

Writing

Before the session, consider the opportunities that you have to form links with other communities, perhaps a church of a different ethnic background whose members meet in your own local area, or a Christian mission organisation working overseas, to which you are linked. Provide writing paper and pens and invite the children to write introductory letters to the other community, as a first step towards forging links with them, which can be followed up over time.

Talk about the way that we are all linked as children of God, no matter what differences there are between us. Discuss the children's thoughts and ideas as they write their letters, and the issues raised.

Prayer and reflective activity

If possible, go out into your local community and sit down together somewhere that you can watch what is going on close by. If you cannot go out to complete this reflection, film some footage of a local area that you can replay to the group.

Talk about the things that you see when you look really closely at your local community. Who or what often passes us by unnoticed? How can we make sure that we do not ignore anyone and the things which they may need?

Challenge

Arrange for one of your leaders, who has the appropriate skills or qualifications, to teach your group some basic first aid skills, perhaps looking at wound dressing, practising on one another.

Talk about the way that the good Samaritan in the story took care of the man he found, tending to his wounds and getting him to a place where he could be looked after.

Prayer

Father God, thank you that we are all your children, known and loved by you. Help us to show love to others, regardless of how different they are from us, so that we can be good neighbours. Amen

Songs

Songs today could include:

- 'You can reach out' (Doug Horley)

Take home

Suggest to the children that they look for an opportunity to show love to somebody else in their community, with their parents' permission, and offer help as needed—walking a dog for a neighbour or baking cakes to take into school, for example.

29 The lost sheep

For the team

Refer to pages 6–9 to see how the activity areas work together

Session theme

This is the first of three sessions exploring the parables of the lost and found, told together by Jesus. In this session, we consider how God is the good shepherd, who cares for us all, his sheep, and how he will do whatever it takes to bring us back to him.

Bible text: Luke 15:4–7

Team prayer

God, our shepherd, thank you for the way that you care for us, your sheep. Help us to celebrate with you when someone who was lost returns to the fold. Amen

Story time

Share the story with the children, either from a Bible or children's Bible story book, perhaps in preparation for the drama activity.

- How does this story make you feel?
- What do we discover about God?
- How should we respond to this story?

Explain to the children that the Bible uses the imagery of God as a shepherd on several different occasions. In this story, we see just how much God loves us: he will search high and low to bring his lost sheep back to him.

Say: I wonder if you've ever felt far from God. I wonder if you know how that sheep felt to be brought back home safely by the shepherd. God loves us so much and does not want us to be separated from him. He wants us all to come back home to him.

Activity areas

Drama

Divide the group into two smaller groups and provide each group with a copy of the passage, either from the Bible or from a children's Bible story book. Ask one group to put together a drama, retelling the story from the perspective of the sheep, and the other group to retell the story from the perspective of the shepherd. Once they have had time to create and rehearse their drama, invite each group to perform their scenes for one another, putting the story together.

Talk about how the story is different when viewed through the eyes of each of the main characters. Ask the children to think about which character from the story they are most able to relate to, and why that is.

ICT

Set up a laptop with a camera and simple motion grabbing software. Provide modelling clay and work with the children to make the models needed, before creating a simple modelling clay stop motion animation which retells the story of the lost sheep.

Talk to the children about what they will do to tell each part of the story to ensure that they include the key details as well as the central message of the parable, which Jesus told. How does telling the story to other people help us to better understand the story ourselves?

Creative

Arrange for one of your leaders, with the appropriate skills, to teach the children the basics of knitting or crocheting, providing suitable tools and wool.

Talk about how we use sheep today both for food and for the wool they provide. In Jesus' time, sheep were also used for sacrifices and would have been valuable to those who cared for them.

Construction

Collect a large supply of old newspapers and challenge the children to use them, and a roll of masking tape, to construct a secure sheepfold. This activity could be organised for children to work in competing teams, with a small prize being awarded to the group who are most successful.

Talk about the way that a shepherd gathers his sheep together to keep them safe from harm and how God cares for us in the same way.

Prayer and reflective activity

Provide printouts of Psalm 23 to look at together with the children. You could also provide large sheets of paper, paint or collaging materials and invite the children to represent the psalm in picture form.

Talk about how this psalm helps us to see God as the good shepherd. What things does he do for his sheep? What does this mean for us?

Games

Set up a sheep trial, where leaders play the role of sheep whom the children can take turns to try to herd, returning them to a sheep pen, perhaps the one constructed from newspaper in the construction activity. You could provide a whistle, or teach the children the directions to use, and perhaps involve another child in playing the part of the sheepdog. Encourage the leaders to be disobedient and troublesome to make this game even more fun!

Challenge

Fill a number of empty plastic bottles with different quantities of small objects, such as marbles, feathers and pebbles. Invite the children to come and estimate how many of the given object there are in each of the bottles.

Talk about the way that the shepherd in the story counted each of his sheep, even though there were 100 of them, and he knew when one was missing. Do we have any collections of things that we value so much that we would immediately notice if one piece was missing?

Prayer

Father God, thank you that you know each of us by name and that we all matter to you. Thank you that no matter where we wander off to, you will always welcome us back and take care of us. Amen

Songs

Songs today could include:

- 'Wrong way' (Dave Godfrey)

Take home

Encourage the children to think about one of their friends who does not yet know Jesus and to begin to pray for them every day, that they would discover who Jesus is, and be reunited with God's family. Encourage the children to share their stories and questions over the coming weeks, reminding them to keep praying for their friends.

30
The lost coin

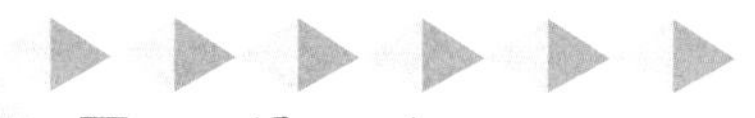

For the team

Refer to pages 6–9 to see how the activity areas work together

Session theme

This session is the second in a series of three, which explores the parables Jesus told about what it means to be lost and found. In this session, we explore how we are like the coin that the woman searched for until it was found again, and how Jesus sees our true value.

Bible text: Luke 15:8–10

Team prayer

Father God, thank you that you know us and love us. Help us to share your heart for the lost, and your great love for all people, so that the children we work with will come to understand what it means to be valued by you. Amen

Story time

Share the story with the children, reading from an appropriate Bible translation or Bible story book. You may wish to read the story together before completing the drama activity.

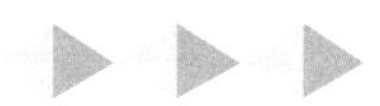

- Why do you think Jesus told this story?
- What does this story add to what we learned in the last session?
- What do we discover about Jesus from this story?
- How does this story help us to understand our relationship with God?

Tell the children that this is one of three stories exploring themes of lost and found that Jesus told to help people to understand how much God loves his people. When we better understand this, we can appreciate how God feels about us and about other people too, and perhaps think about the way that we show love to others.

Say: I wonder whether we know what it means to be loved and found by God. I wonder what we can do to share God's love with other people who do not know him. Just as the woman went searching for her lost coin, God wants us to be reunited with him.

Drama

Challenge the children to create a modern-day retelling of the parable of the lost coin. Ask them to think about where their retelling would take place, who the main character would be, and what would be the modern-day, precious object equivalent of the lost coin. You could provide a selection of props which the children can use as they put together their sketch.

Talk about the children's own ideas for retelling this story in a modern context and how they can explore the same themes as the original text. How does retelling the story help us to better understand the parable? How precious would the woman's coin have been to her?

ICT

Using a design or paint programme, invite the children to design their own coin of a value of their choosing. Provide a number of coins of different values or pictures of coins if appropriate. These could include historic coins or foreign coins, from which the children can gather ideas before creating their own coin.

Talk about how precious the woman's coin was to her. She must have known every detail it had on it.

Creative

Collect a selection of small pieces of fabric and provide sewing needles, thread and scissors. Invite the children to use the materials provided to create their own small purse or wallet which they can use to store precious coins. You could also provide press-studs or small buttons and cord which can be used to seal the purse securely.

Talk about where the woman may have kept her coins. There is no mention of a purse or a piggy bank, but she clearly wanted to keep her coins safe, because she spent so much time looking for the one she lost.

Construction

If possible, involve your group in gathering resources that are easily found in your local area (such as leaves and twigs from a town park, driftwood, shells and rolled glass from a beach, or fallen branches and stones from a wood). Invite the children to work with you to construct a sculpture or piece of art from the items that they have found.

Talk about how it feels to find something that is precious to you. How is discovering something for the first time different from finding something that you had lost?

Books

Books provided could include children's Bibles and story books that retell a selection of Jesus' parables.

Talk about the things that interest the children when they look at the books, as appropriate, and be available to support those less able to read independently.

Prayer and reflective activity

Gather some old pennies and fill a glass with a cola drink. Drop a penny into the cola and invite the children to watch as it cleans the coin.

Talk about the fact that the coin has the same value whether it is clean or dirty. Ask the children what they think this means for the way that Jesus sees and values us.

Games

Set up a treasure hunt in your venue, perhaps for chocolate coins or sparkly 'gems', which the children can hunt for and gather together.

Prayer

Dear Jesus, thank you for the way that we can learn from the stories that you used to teach people. Thank you that through this story we can discover what it means to be known, valued and loved by you. Amen

Songs

Songs today could include:

- 'King of love' (Doug Horley)

Take home

Give each of the children a shiny penny to take home with them as a reminder of the story explored in this session and how much God values them.

31

The prodigal son

For the team

Refer to pages 6–9 to see how the activity areas work together

Session theme

In this final session in the trilogy of lost and found stories, we explore the experiences of the two brothers and how we can relate to them, whether we feel close to God or far away. In this session, we celebrate Father God's great gifts of love and forgiveness available to us all.

Bible text: Luke 15:11–32

Team prayer

Father God, thank you for loving us all the same, whether we stay by your side or travel far from home. May we celebrate with you when your children come back home. Amen

Story time

Use an age-appropriate children's translation of the Bible to read the story together, or refer to the text as you work together as a group to complete the drama activity, as detailed below.

- What did you enjoy most about this story?
- What surprised you?
- Could you recognise any of the characters in yourself or people you know?
- Did anything in this story make you stop and think?

Explain to the group that the dad in this story represents God, our heavenly Father who loves us no matter what we do. Ask the children to think about the two sons in the story—the older son who stayed with his dad and worked hard for him, but didn't understand how his dad could love and forgive his brother, and the younger son who took his dad's money and spent the lot, before his dad forgave him and welcomed him back home.

Say: I wonder whether you feel close to God, like the older brother, or whether you feel as though God is far away, like the younger brother in the story. God loves you and wants to celebrate you being in his family too.

Activity areas

Drama

Invite the children to create a series of freeze frames, depicting scenes from the story. Have a Bible available to decide which scenes to depict and to help decide which details to include in each of the scenes. You could provide a selection of appropriate costumes and simple props for the children to use.

Talk about what is happening in each stage of the story as they work through the narrative. Can they imagine how the story could have worked out differently?

ICT

Photograph the freeze frames (created previously) and upload them into a word processing programme. Add speech or thought bubbles for the children to type their own ideas about what the character may be thinking or saying at each point in the story.

Talk about the children's ideas for the characters' thoughts and conversations at each point in the story. Refer back to the original story to ensure that you remain faithful to it, and use the opportunity to talk about the surprising events as they occur.

Creative

Provide a selection of catalogues and magazines, as well as plain paper, glue and scissors. Invite the children to imagine how they might spend £1000, to create a 'spent it all' collage.

Talk about the way that the younger son attracted lots of friends when he had money to spend, but that when the money was gone, the friends disappeared too. We think that having lots of money will make us happy, but as the son in the story found, this isn't true.

Construction

Gather a large quantity of newspapers and rolls of masking tape, and ask the children to construct a pen to keep the pigs in by rolling the newspapers to make 'sticks' which can then be put together. If you have a larger group, you could split them into smaller teams and set up a pig-pen building competition.

Talk about how the son in the story had to look after the pigs when all his money had gone, and how this was considered the worst job he could have had.

Writing

Offer paper and pens and pencils and invite the children to write a letter from the father in the story while the son is away from home, telling him how much he is missed and loved and how he would like his son to come back home again.

Talk about the way that the son was completely oblivious to how much his dad was missing him, until he arrived home. Explain that, at the time of Jesus, it was far more difficult than it is today to keep in touch with a person who had left home.

Books

Display a variety of age-appropriate children's Bibles and story books telling the story of the prodigal son.

Talk about the things that interest the children when they look at the books, as appropriate, and be available to support those less able to read independently.

Prayer and reflective activity

On a large sheet of paper write, 'God is the Perfect Dad' and provide post-it notes and pens. Invite the children to think about God as the perfect dad, and to write their ideas on the post-it notes, before sticking them on to the paper. Comments may include 'always loves us' or 'is always there'.

Talk about the children's ideas as they add them to the paper, and sensitively discuss any issues that may arise as children consider their own experiences or relationships with their fathers. Help them to understand that Father God will never fail us.

Games

Set up a simple scavenger hunt where the children have to search for objects relating to the story. This could include some coins, a toy pig, a ring and a coat.

Talk about the way that the son left home and was lost to his family, but returned home again, safe and sound.

Prayer

Father God, thank you that no matter where we go or what we do, you love us as your children and want to welcome us into your family. There is nothing that we can do that you won't forgive, because you love us. Amen

Songs

Songs today could include:

- 'Father God I wonder' (Ishmael)
- 'Open arms (Prodigal song)' (Andy Flannagan)

Take home

Suggest that the children spend some time in the week ahead talking about this story with their families. What does it mean for them to be loved by Father God?

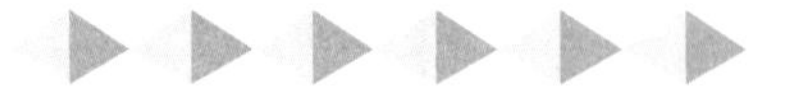

32 Jesus notices Zacchaeus

For the team

Refer to pages 6–9 to see how the activity areas work together

Session theme

Through this session, we discover more about God's topsy-turvy kingdom, where Jesus surprised the crowds by mixing with the most unlikely of people. In this session, we consider the way that we are changed when we meet with Jesus, and how we then live differently, just as Zacchaeus did.

Bible text: Luke 19:1–10

Team prayer

Dear Jesus, thank you that you extend an invitation to all people to meet with you. Thank you for the way our lives have been changed by that meeting. Help us to extend that invitation to the children we work with today, that they too may encounter you for themselves. Amen

Story time

Share the story with the children, perhaps retelling the story or reading it together from an appropriate Bible translation or children's story Bible. This could be done in preparation for the drama activity, as described below.

- How does this story make you feel?
- What surprises you most?
- How would Zacchaeus' perspective on what happened have been different from the crowd's perspective?
- How does this story challenge us to respond?

Remind the children that the crowds were sometimes shocked by the types of people that Jesus spent time with. Jesus explained, though, that he had come to earth to reach out to the neediest people, not those who had everything 'sorted' in their lives.

Say: I wonder what Jesus might say to us if we were to meet him. The people who met Jesus would be forever changed by their encounters with him, as Zacchaeus was. He changed his life around completely. I wonder how Jesus might change our lives.

Drama

Invite a confident volunteer to play the part of Zacchaeus and to sit in the hot seat. The rest of the group can then interview Zacchaeus, asking him any questions about what happened to him when he encountered Jesus. Encourage Zacchaeus to remain in role, ad libbing his responses as appropriate to the questions asked.

Talk about the different questions the children can ask Zacchaeus and the responses given by Zacchaeus, along with any issues raised by the children's ideas.

ICT

Set up a laptop or computer with access to a printer and an appropriate design programme. Invite the children to create their own invitations and print them out. Provide envelopes for them to use to give their invitation to a friend. You may have a special event coming up which the children can invite their friends to, or simply print invitations for your next group session.

Talk about how we feel when we receive an invitation. Jesus became Zacchaeus' most special guest, but Zacchaeus had no idea, when the day began, that he would be hosting Jesus for tea.

Construction

Provide the appropriate materials and tools for the children, working with the help of an adult, to build or perhaps upcycle a table together. This could be a construction project with wood, hammers and nails, or an upcycling activity involving making repairs to an old table and painting or decorating it to create a finished product.

Talk about the way that Jesus chose to spend time with Zacchaeus, sitting down for a meal with him, and how that changed his life. How can you use this table to share time with other people in the same way and create a special place where people can discover more about Jesus?

Books

Along with books which retell the story of Zacchaeus and age-appropriate children's Bibles, you could provide some books including detailed illustrations or puzzles that children need to look at closely. Examples might be 'spot the difference' pictures, or books such as *Where's Wally?*

Share the books with the children, supporting them with reading as needed. Talk about the way that Jesus noticed Zacchaeus even though he was trying to remain out of the way.

Prayer and reflective activity

Provide some chocolate coins for the children to take away to share with other people. Encourage them to use this as an opportunity to tell their friends that God loves them, and to tell them about the story of Zacchaeus and how Jesus changed his life.

Talk about the way Zacchaeus chose to give away so much of his money after he met Jesus. How can Jesus change our lives too?

Games

Games which involve making changes would work well today, reminding the children of the changes that Zacchaeus made. One suggestion would be to play a game where a volunteer is asked to leave the room while one or two members of the rest of the group make subtle changes to their appearance, perhaps taking off a jacket or swapping a shoe with another child. When the volunteer returns to the room, they should try to work out what has changed among the other players.

Challenge

If possible, go out into the local area and find some appropriate trees for the children to climb, in the same way that Zacchaeus climbed the sycamore tree to get a better view of Jesus. You will need to carry out a risk assessment in advance, to identify and manage the risks involved, and seek parental permission for the activity. Alternatively, supervise the children as they use a climbing frame in a local park

Talk about how the children feel when they are up in the tree or on the climbing frame: protected or vulnerable? How do you think Zacchaeus felt?

Prayer

Dear Jesus, thank you for the way that you changed Zacchaeus' life when you invited him to join you for tea. Thank you that you invite us to join you too, and that we too can be changed by that meeting. Amen

Songs

Songs today could include:

- 'Your eyes' (David Wakerly, Beci Wakerly and Julia A'Bell)

Take home

Challenge the children to do one kind or generous thing for someone else this week, as Zacchaeus did when he gave his money away. Encourage them to look for opportunities to talk to their friends about the way that Jesus has changed their lives.

33

Palm Sunday

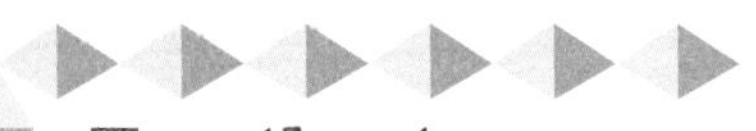

For the team

Refer to pages 6–9 to see how the activity areas work together

Session theme

This session retells what happened at the start of Holy Week, when Jesus the king entered the city of Jerusalem. We look back on those events knowing how the story will end, but the activities of this session are designed to look at Palm Sunday with fresh eyes, joining the crowds on that day as they celebrated the arrival of their king.

Bible text: Matthew 21:1–11; Luke 19:28–44

Team prayer

Welcome, King Jesus, into our lives! May we never forget that you are the true king, higher than all earthly authorities, who entered the city on a lowly donkey. Amen

Story time

Share the story with the children, either reading from a Bible or a children's Bible story book. You may like to provide copies of the text for the children to look at as you do so, in preparation for the drama activity.

- How does this story make you feel?
- What do you think it would have been like to be there in the crowds?
- Why were the onlookers so surprised by events at the time?
- What surprises you most about this story?

Remind the children that this episode came towards the end of Jesus' time on earth, but the crowds looking on did not know that. Explain that God's people had been waiting for the arrival of the saviour, as king of their people. But their expectations were different (perhaps more in line with what we may have expected) from what Jesus actually did that day and what followed after that.

Say: I wonder why God chose to do things this way. I wonder what this tells us about God and his kingdom. This story marks the beginning of the most important week, in which we see God's big story reaching a great climax. Jesus is the king of kings, who turned the world on its head to bring in his kingdom.

Activity areas

Drama

Divide the children into two small groups. Ask one group to create a short drama or freeze frame to show how you might expect a king to arrive into a city, and the other group to show how Jesus arrived into the city of Jerusalem. Ask the groups to perform their scenes alongside one another, so that they can be seen in direct comparison.

Talk about the differences that the children notice between the two scenes. Ask the children if they notice anything in common between the two scenes. Remind the children that Jesus is the king of kings, but that he came in a way nobody could have expected.

ICT

Gather some small people figures and a toy donkey, along with props to illustrate the setting for Palm Sunday, including trees, city walls, coats and leaves (perhaps made of paper or felt). Set up a laptop with a camera and appropriate motion grabbing software to create a simple animation of Jesus on his way into Jerusalem. Once images have been captured, you could add sound effects over the top, with the crowd cheering for Jesus.

Talk about how we can represent the important parts of the story in this animation sequence, to ensure that we retell the story effectively and capture the significance of events.

Creative

Provide some palm crosses to show the children and long strips of sugar paper. Work with the children to construct a palm cross by folding the paper strips. (You can find instructions online—for example, at www.youtube.com/watch?v=JcmeCOf-b4k.) This activity may work well in smaller groups, in order to ensure that the children are supported at each stage of the construction.

Talk about the way that palm crosses have become a familiar image to us, but on that first Palm Sunday the crowds could not have predicted how the story would end. They thought this was a great time of celebration.

Construction

Source an old trailer or pram chassis that can be used to create a royal carriage, using a selection of appropriate scrap materials and tools, together with metallic paint and decorative items. You could provide some photographs of royal carriages as a stimulus for the children's construction activities.

Talk about the way that Jesus arrived in Jerusalem, not in a royal horse-drawn carriage, as you might expect, but on a lowly donkey. Why is this so surprising? Why is this an important detail in the story?

Books

Set out on display a selection of children's story books which retell the story of Jesus' time on earth, particularly those which retell the events of Palm Sunday and Holy Week, as well as age-appropriate Bibles.

Share the books with the children, offering to support those who need help with reading, and helping the children to recap the events of Jesus' life which led up to the events of this week.

Prayer and reflective activity

Show news footage of a royal visit; where possible, one local to your group. This could include news footage on a laptop, newspaper reports and photographs.

Talk about how different Jesus' visit to Jerusalem was in comparison to our royal visits. There were no special vehicles, just a donkey. No media to hold interviews and film the events, no security guards or fancy clothes. But there were great crowds of people who wanted to welcome and praise Jesus as he arrived.

Games

Games today could include a donkey race, where children work in pairs, one as the donkey, kneeling on all fours, with a rider sat on their back. This could be done as a team relay race, under appropriate supervision to ensure safety.

Prayer

Hosanna, King Jesus! We welcome you into our lives. Amen

Songs

Songs today could include:

- 'Blessed is he who comes' (Dave Godfrey)
- 'Hosanna' (Carl Tuttle)

Take home

Invite the children to take home a palm cross, either the ones they made in the creative activity or perhaps those made from a palm leaf. Encourage the children to display their palm cross somewhere at home, where the whole family can see it, and remember the events of the week to come.

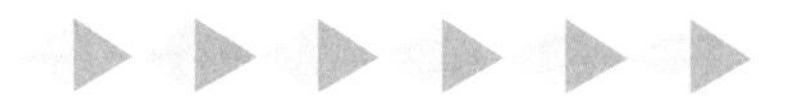

34

A very sad day and a very happy day

For the team

Refer to pages 6–9 to see how the activity areas work together

Session theme

This session explores the most central episode of God's story—Jesus' death and resurrection, preceded by the events of Holy Week. Through this session, we explore some of the emotions attached to the story and how, ultimately, through these events we can know true joy.

Bible text: Matthew 26—28

Team prayer

Lord Jesus, thank you for the sacrifice that you made, and for your gifts of freedom, forgiveness and fresh starts. Help us to share our joy with the children with whom we work—a joy won by your victory on the cross. Amen

Story time

Today's story can be explored and retold through the events of the drama activity, or by holding up the collage boards as made in today's creative activity. It may work more effectively to summarise the story to share with the children, rather than reading directly from the Bible.

- How does this story make you feel?
- What is your favourite part?
- How do you think we should respond to this story?
- Does this story raise any new questions for you?

Explain to the children that this is the most important part of God's big story. Since the time when Adam and Eve first made a bad decision, God had been working things together to make a way for human beings to have a good and right relationship with him once again. Through Jesus' death and resurrection, we have a way back to God and that gives us something to be really happy about.

Discuss any issues and questions raised by the story, and be ready to help the children to respond to the things they have heard, as appropriate. There may be specific things that require following up with the children today, so perhaps have some leaders available to help with this throughout the session.

Activity areas

Drama

Provide copies of the text, or children's Bibles, and look together at the events in today's story. Highlight the different emotions that each of the characters would have felt, and ask the children to show each of these emotions through their facial expressions and body language, as you read the text.

Talk about how we can look at the story as a whole, knowing how it will end, but Jesus' followers could not do that. They experienced the unfolding events one after another, without knowing what would happen next, so the emotions they were feeling would have been strong and real.

Creative

Provide large card or foam boards, along with pens, paints and a selection of collaging materials. Invite the children to create one collaged display board to represent each of the key events of Holy Week and Easter to tell the story.

Talk about which events from the story the children want to portray on each of the boards and how they will do so pictorially.

ICT

Use a digital camera to photograph the completed collage boards from the 'Creative' activity, detailing the events of Holy Week. Use the photos to create a PowerPoint presentation, perhaps adding text or sounds to retell the story.

Talk about why this story is so important to us, and how we can share it creatively with other people. How could you share the PowerPoint file with others, as a way of telling the story?

Construction

Work together with the children to create a large model of the tomb and surrounding garden. Chicken wire can be used to construct a basic frame which can then be covered in Modroc or papier mâché, before painting to create an appropriate stone effect.

Talk about how the tomb, which should be such a sad place, has become a symbol of celebration for us, as Christians, as we always use the empty tomb to remind us that Jesus overcame death.

Writing

Provide a selection of Easter cards, or perhaps print out some photographs of the collaged boards which can be used as a card, along with pens and envelopes, and invite the children to write a message in a card to send to someone else, perhaps to tell them something about the Easter story.

Talk about the different messages that we can write. How do we share the good news of the Easter story with our friends and family members?

Books

Provide a selection of Bibles and age-appropriate children's books which retell the events of the Easter story.

Share the books with the children, supporting them with reading as necessary and talking about how each of the story books retells the events of Easter.

Prayer and reflective activity

Provide a large wooden cross, small pieces of paper, nails and lightweight hammers. Invite the children to write their name on a piece of paper, before nailing it to the cross, with help and supervision as needed, as a sign of accepting that Jesus died for us.

Talk about what it means, in an age-appropriate way, for Jesus to have taken our place on the cross and what the children understand this to mean.

Prayer

Dear Jesus, thank you that you died on the cross, and that you were resurrected, beating death, so we could be your friends once again. Amen

Songs

Songs today could include:

- 'All through history' (Becky Drake)
- 'Resurrection' (Dave Godfrey)

Take home

Encourage the children to take their Easter cards away with them and to give these to one of their friends, to tell them something about Jesus and the story of Easter.

35

Jesus returns to heaven

For the team

Refer to pages 6–9 to see how the activity areas work together

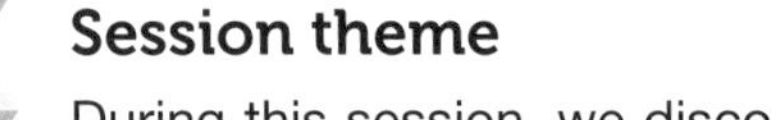

Session theme

During this session, we discover what happened when Jesus returned to heaven and explore how we, like the first disciples of Jesus, can live out Jesus' final command to be his witnesses to all the ends of the earth.

Bible text: Acts 1:6–11

Team prayer

Lord Jesus, thank you that you walked on earth, demonstrating how to live life in a God-honouring way. May we continue to share your story with all those we meet, and encourage the children with whom we work to do the same. Amen

Story time

Use an appropriate Bible translation or a children's Bible story book to look at the Bible passage for this session, encouraging the children to try to imagine the events as you read.

- Why do you think, after everything that had happened, Jesus returned to heaven?
- How do you think the disciples would have felt about this?
- How do you think they would have felt once Jesus had left them?
- What do we discover about God from this story?

Explain to the children that Jesus was resurrected from the dead, to conquer or beat death. That completed his work on earth and he could then return to heaven, as he had already told the disciples he would do, once his work was finished.

Say: I wonder how we might feel if we had to say goodbye to Jesus, as the disciples did. Thanks to Jesus' resurrection and ascension, he can live within us and work through us, even though we will not see him face to face, until we are reunited with him. You may wish to explore this idea in further detail with the children.

Drama

Define an area in which the children can move about to participate in this drama activity. Ask the children to move around within the space, and listen for a given signal, such as a small bell or whistle. On hearing the signal, the children should turn to the person closest to them and re-enact a greeting or parting, with the appropriate gestures, and things to say to one another. Continue this activity, repeating with several meetings and departures, encouraging the children to use different ways of saying hello or goodbye to the other children, as they interact.

Talk about the different times when we meet and greet someone, or say goodbye, and the different emotions linked to these interactions. Explain that this story is all about one great departure, as Jesus returned to heaven.

ICT

Set up a laptop or tablet with the means to email or, if possible, use Voice over IP (such as Skype) to communicate with a missionary linked to your church community. Use this as an opportunity to find out more about what the missionary you are connected to does in the place where they are working.

Talk about how Jesus told his followers they would be his witnesses throughout the world. For some people, like the missionaries you are connected to, this means travelling many miles to do so. Talk about the issues that are raised by your conversation with a missionary, and what else you can do to pray for and support the person or family involved.

Creative

Gather a variety of collage materials along with pieces of coloured card, envelopes and pens. Invite the children to create a 'Welcome' or 'Sorry you are leaving' card, as they wish, to a friend or family member as appropriate, or perhaps to a new member of the group.

Talk about how we feel about people coming and going, arriving or departing. The disciples had only just celebrated Jesus being returned to them after his death and resurrection, and now he was physically leaving them for the final time. How do you think they felt?

Construction

Provide cardboard boxes, along with card and other craft materials, including glue and scissors. Invite the children to create their own room box out of the cardboard box, making furniture from the other provided materials. Encourage the children to design their own dream room, including all the things they would most like to have in their own home.

Talk about the time when Jesus told his disciples that he would return to heaven to prepare a place for them, a special forever home (see John 14:2–3). Ask them to consider whether they think our home in heaven will be anything like we expect; what do you think Jesus would be doing to prepare a home for us?

Books

Along with the Bibles and children's Bibles offered today, set out a few atlases for the children to look at. Encourage them to search for places which are familiar to them, as well as more obscure places which perhaps they have not heard of before. Explain that Jesus' followers began the task of sharing his message around the world—a task his followers still take up today.

Talk about the things that interest the children when they look at the books, as appropriate, and be available to support those less able to read independently.

Prayer and reflective activity

Provide a number of different maps and atlases, including a map of your local area, a world map and a map of the Holy Land which shows the places Jesus mentioned in his message to the disciples. Give the children stickers to use to mark the places mentioned by Jesus, before looking at the other maps. Invite the children to mark places on these maps where you have the opportunity to spread Jesus' message, on both an international and a local scale.

Talk about the different connections your group have, both internationally and locally, and pray for the opportunities that these connections provide for you to be witnesses for Jesus.

Games

Provide paper and work with the children to explore how to make the best paper aeroplanes before challenging them to make a paper aeroplane of their choice. Hold a competition to see which plane flies the furthest, perhaps awarding a small prize to the winner. Remind the children that Jesus sent his followers far and wide to share his story with the world.

Prayer

Dear Jesus, thank you for your story, thank you for those who shared your story with us, and thank you that we can take our turn in sharing your story with others too. Amen

Songs

Songs today could include:

- 'Go' (Dave Godfrey)

Take home

Challenge the children to consider who they will meet in the week ahead and how they can share a little of Jesus' story with those people. Encourage them to pray that God would give them opportunities to be witnesses for him, and to ask for the courage to take those opportunities. Invite the children to share their experiences at the next session.

36

God sends his helper

For the team

Refer to pages 6–9 to see how the activity areas work together

Session theme

In this final session, we discover what happened when the Holy Spirit settled on the first disciples at Pentecost, enabling and equipping them to do more than they could ever have imagined. Through this session, we discover more about the Holy Spirit and how we too can receive his gifts, equipping us to live out our faith and to play our part in God's story.

Bible text: Acts 2

Team prayer

Come, Holy Spirit, and fill us once again with your power to do your work among your people. Amen

Story time

Provide access to Bibles or a children's Bible story book for the children to look at this story together. Since this is a fairly long chapter, you may wish to summarise elements of the story, as you look at it together with the children.

- Who do you think was most surprised by the events of this day?
- What surprises you most about this story?
- How does this story conclude God's big story?
- In what ways is this story only the beginning?

Explain that when this story happened, Jesus' disciples were feeling very frightened and uncertain about what might happen to them, and what they would do now that Jesus had gone. Jesus' time on earth had come to an end, but the disciples' work was just beginning. In this story, we discover how the Holy Spirit came upon the disciples, equipping and enabling them to do his work.

Say: I wonder what it would have been like to be among the disciples on that day. The Holy Spirit descended on them in a very visual way. The same Holy Spirit comes into each of our lives when we choose to become a follower of Jesus, equipping and enabling us to do more than we could ever imagine.

Drama

Provide access to Bibles, or retellings of the story, and work together with the children to create a news report, assigning some children the role of reporters, while others can play the parts of some of the disciples who were involved in the events of Pentecost. Others can be eyewitnesses to events, perhaps talking about how they heard the disciples talking in their home languages. You could use a digital camera to film the report, ready to view later.

Talk about the details that the children want to include in the news report. Who would they most like to interview? What questions would the interviewers want the interviewees to answer?

ICT

Provide safe access to the internet, using tablets or laptops, and invite the children to use a reliable translation website to translate words and phrases of interest to them into different languages. The children could use this time to look at the phrase, 'Come, Holy Spirit', among other phrases to use in the writing activity below. Encourage the children to look at languages relevant to the group, perhaps those spoken by friends and family members of the group.

Talk about the different languages that the children choose to look at and practise pronunciation as appropriate. Do any members of your group speak English as an additional language? How do they feel when they hear their first language spoken?

Creative

Provide large card or foam boards and a selection of different collaging materials, glue, pens and scissors. Work with the children to create a number of different collage boards, each showing a different scene, to tell the key events of God's story from creation to Pentecost.

Talk about the way that the events of Pentecost enabled many, many more people to hear God's story for the first time, and in turn these stories have been passed on to us. How can we take our turn in sharing these stories with other people?

Construction

Provide some lengths of wood and the appropriate woodworking equipment which the children can use, under supervision, to work safely together to build a small, sturdy platform.

Talk about the way that Peter stood in front of the crowd and shared God's story with them. We may not stand on a stage to talk to people about God, but what different 'platforms' do we have where we can share God's story?

Writing

Provide small pieces of coloured paper and coloured felt pens. Invite the children to write out the phrase 'Come, Holy Spirit', in different languages on each piece of paper. Encourage the children to use different handwriting styles too and use the completed strips of paper to create a display.

Talk about the way that all the strips of paper share something common, holding the same message, but all in different languages and writing styles. On the day when the Holy Spirit was sent to God's people, everyone was held together, able to hear the same message, but each in their own languages.

Books

Display a selection of children's Bibles and books which retell the story of Pentecost for the children to read. You could also provide a selection of books which explore more about the person and gifts of the Holy Spirit.

Talk about the things that interest the children when they look at the books, as appropriate, and be available to support those less able to read independently.

Prayer and reflective activity

Prepare a number of presents, wrapping boxes in gift wrap and attaching gift labels to each one. Alongside these, provide Bibles or printouts of 1 Corinthians 12:8–11. Invite the children to write their name on one of the gift tags as a sign of accepting God's gift of the Holy Spirit, in the same way that the first disciples did.

Talk about how God enabled the disciples to speak out, by giving them the Holy Spirit who enabled them to speak with confidence in languages they had never spoken before. What could the Holy Spirit enable us to do, if we accept his gifts?

Prayer

Holy Spirit, thank you that you give us all different gifts so that we can better share God's story with the people we know. Help us as we discover more about the gifts that you have for us. Amen

Songs

Songs today could include:

- 'On the day of Pentecost' (Dave Godfrey)
- 'When Peter preached' (Dave Godfrey)

Take home

Provide copies of 1 Corinthians 12:8–11 for the children to take home with them. Encourage the children to think about where they see these gifts in the lives of other followers of God, and what he enables them to do, and to pray about the gifts that God may have given to them.

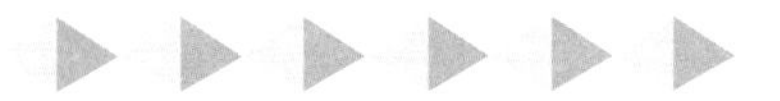

Templates

All templates can be downloaded at www.barnabasinchurches.org.uk/9780857464262

Advent calendar

1	2	3	4
5	6	7	8
9	10	11	12
13	14	15	16
17	18	19	20
21	22	23	24

Jointed person

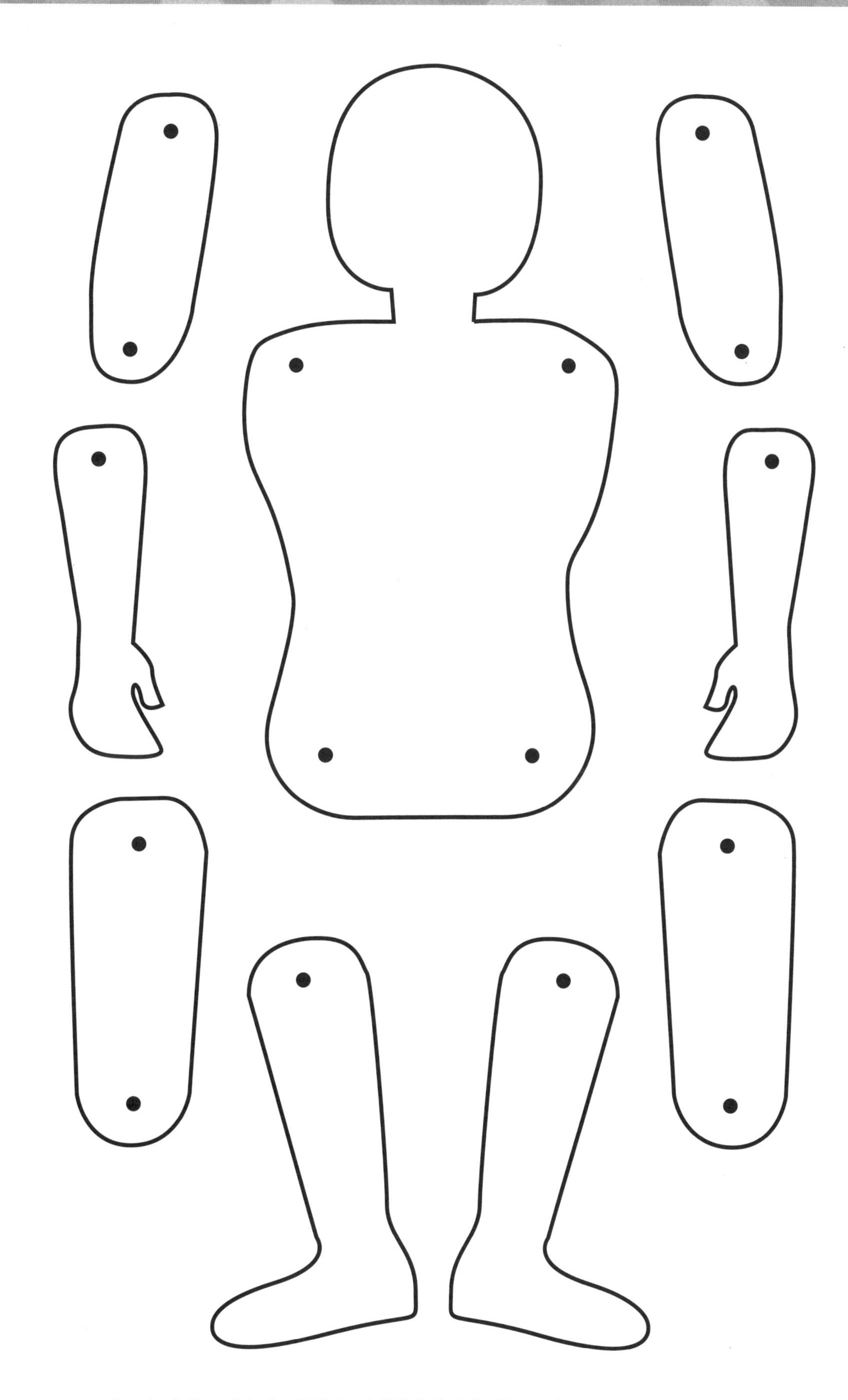

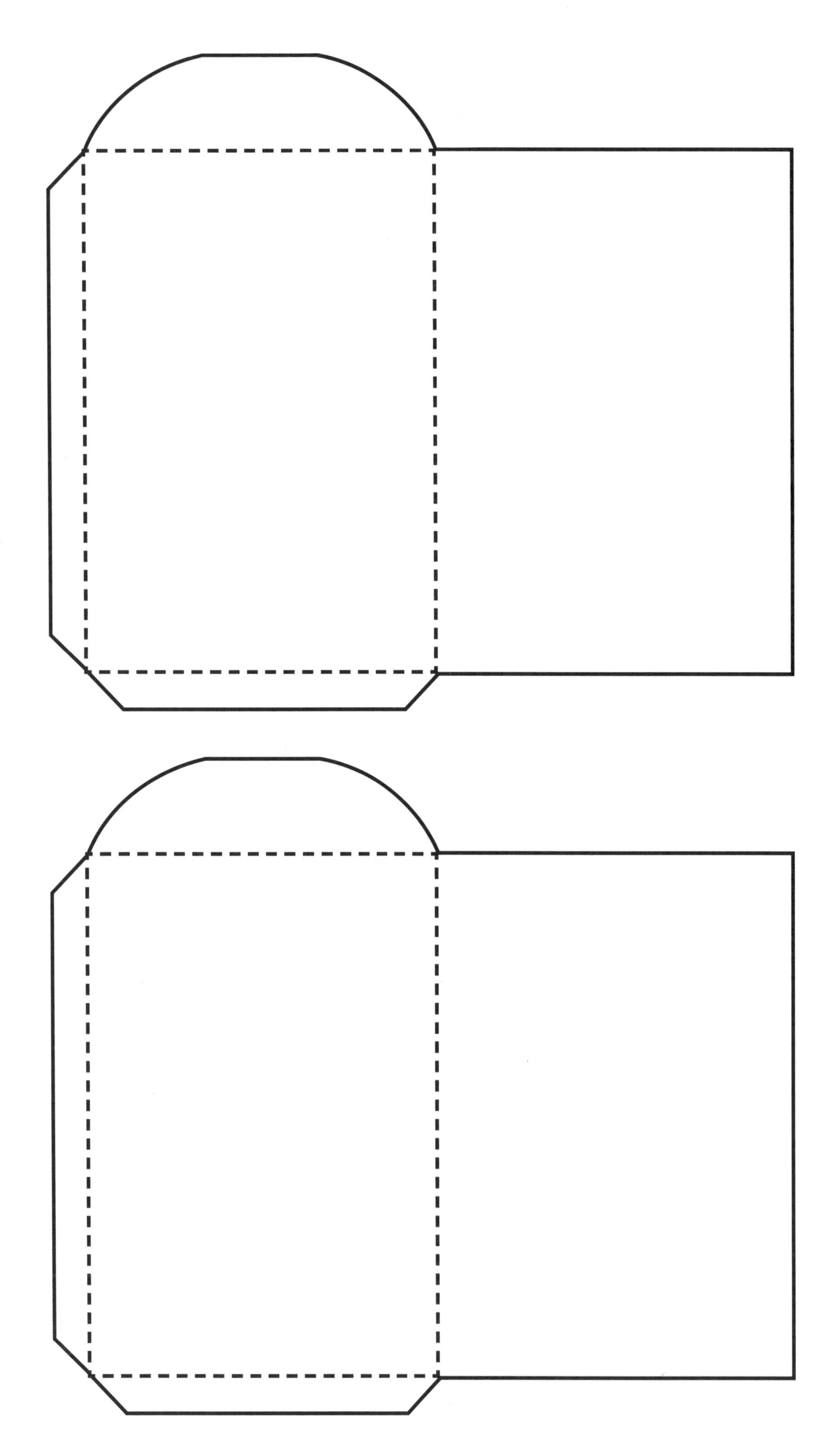

